D0474358

Color Correction with

DAVINCI RESOLVE 15

by Daria Fissoun

Color Correction with DaVinci Resolve 15

Daria Fissoun

Copyright © 2019 by Blackmagic Design Pty Ltd

Blackmagic Design

www.blackmagicdesign.com

To report errors, please send a note to learning@blackmagicdesign.com.

Contributing authors: Jason Druss, Mary Plummer, Dion Scoppettuolo, David Hover

Series Editor: Patricia Montesion

Editor: Bob Lindstrom

Cover Design: Blackmagic Design

Notice of Rights

All rights reserved. No part of this book may be reproduced or transmitted in any form by any means, electronic, mechanical, photocopying, recording, or otherwise, without the prior written permission of the publisher. For information on getting permission for reprints and excerpts, contact learning@blackmagicdesign.com.

Notice of Liability

Neither the author nor Blackmagic Design shall have any liability to any person or entity for any loss or damage caused or alleged to be caused directly or indirectly by the information contained in this book, or by omissions from this book, or by the computer software and hardware products described within it.

Trademarks

Many of the designations used by manufacturers and sellers to distinguish their products are claimed as trademarks. Where those designations appear in this book, and Blackmagic Design was aware of a trademark claim, the designations appear as requested by the owner of the trademark. All other product names and services identified throughout this book are used in editorial fashion only and for the benefit of such companies with no intention of infringement of the trademark. No such use, or the use of any trade name, is intended to convey endorsement or other affiliation with this book.

macOS is a registered trademark of Apple Inc., registered in the U.S. and other countries. Windows is a registered trademarks of Microsoft Inc., registered in the U.S. and other countries.

ISBN: 978-1-7327569-3-9

Contents

Foreword

Welcome to **Color Correction with DaVinci Resolve 15**

I think one of the most exciting things about DaVinci Resolve 15 is that it brings editing, color correction, audio post and now visual effects together in the same software application! With the addition of the new Fusion page in DaVinci Resolve 15, you get over 250 tools for advanced node based visual effects compositing and motion graphics, along with even better color correction and editing features and a full blown Fairlight digital audio workstation. That means you'll be able to switch between creative tasks without having to export or translate files between different applications!

Best of all, DaVinci Resolve 15 is absolutely free! Plus, we've made sure that the free version of DaVinci Resolve actually has more features than any paid editing system. That's because at Blackmagic Design we believe everybody should have the tools to create professional, Hollywood caliber content without having to spend thousands of dollars.

I hope you'll enjoy using DaVinci Resolve 15 and we can't wait to see the amazing work you produce!

Grant Petty
Blackmagic Design

Getting Started

Welcome to **Color Correction with DaVinci Resolve 15**, an official Blackmagic Design-certified training book that teaches professionals and students how to get the most out of color correction using DaVinci Resolve 15. All you need is a Mac or Windows computer, the free download version of Resolve 15, and a passion to learn about color correction.

This guide blends practical, hands-on exercises with the aesthetics of the colorist's art to help you discover new techniques for whatever tasks you take on. You will learn how to use the program's many grading tools and workflows, and gain an in-depth understanding of advanced techniques and creative industry practices. Some exercises will even take you into the realm of compositing, which is an increasingly requested skill of contemporary colorists.

After completing this book, you are encouraged to take the 50-question online proficiency exam to receive a Certificate of Completion from Blackmagic Design. The link to the exam is located at the end of this book.

About DaVinci Resolve 15

DaVinci Resolve is the world's fastest growing and most advanced editing software. It also has a long history of being the world's most trusted application for color correction. In addition to its world-class color correction toolset, DaVinci Resolve 15 is a professional-level non-linear editing and effects application with a complete set of professional audio editing and mixing tools that enable you to complete projects using only one piece of software!

What you will Learn

In these lessons, you'll work with multiple projects to learn advanced, practical techniques used in several editing genres. You'll acquire real-world skills that you can apply to real-world productions.

Part I

Part I of the book will have you restoring a documentary edit from a Resolve archive file. The three lessons within this section focus on fundamental grading theory and practices. You will normalize and balance footage with the primary grading tools in lesson 1, match the shots in the timeline for continuity in lesson 2, and adopt secondary grading workflows in lesson 3.

Part II

Part II looks at more advanced approaches to the grade node structure in the context of a feature film trailer. In Lesson 4, you will migrate the project to Resolve using an XML file format. In Lesson 5, you will more fully explore the importance of node order and consider incorporating mixer nodes when grading to ensure the optimal color outcome. In lesson 6, you will practice different methods of managing and copying grades, with an eye toward developing efficient, quick workflows.

Part III

Part III will focus more strongly on the optimization of grading workflows to ensure a quick, accurate grading process and output. In lesson 7, you will look at a variety of methods of controlling the image frame and properties, as well as advanced keyframing, compositing, and noise-reduction techniques. Lesson 8 will incorporate the classic grading workflow into a group-based pipeline that will allow you to grade entire segments of the timeline in one node tree. Lesson 9 will demonstrate the many approaches you could take when starting a grading workflow with RAW media and emphasize its extended grading potential. Finally, lesson 10 will cover project delivery from basic preset setup to custom renders and DCP workflows.

The appendices at the end of the book provide additional information regarding the layout and functionality of the program, as well as the corresponding controls on the Blackmagic Design Mini Panel.

System Requirements

This book teaches Resolve 15 for macOS and Windows. If you have an older version of DaVinci Resolve, you must upgrade to the current version to follow along with the lessons. Fortunately, DaVinci Resolve 15 is a free upgrade from previous versions of DaVinci Resolve.

Downloading DaVinci Resolve 15

You can download the free version of DaVinci Resolve 15 from the Blackmagic Design website:

1   Open a web browser on your macOS, Windows, or Linux computer.
2   In the address field of your web browser, enter
     www.blackmagicdesign.com/products/davinciresolve.
3   On the DaVinci Resolve landing page, click the Download button.
4   Follow the installation instructions to complete the installation.

When you have completed the software installation, follow the instructions in the following section, "To download and install the lesson files," to download the content for this book.

Acquiring the Lesson Files

You must download three zipped lesson files to acquire the media files you'll use while performing the exercises in this book. After you download and save the compressed files to your hard disk, extract both zipped files and copy them to a single "BMD 15 - Advanced Color Correction" folder that you create in your Documents folder.

To Download and Install the Lesson Files:

When you are ready to download the three lesson files, follow these steps:

1   Connect to the Internet and navigate to:
     www.blackmagicdesign.com/dvres/grading-with-resolve15-pt1.
     The download will begin immediately.

     The "BMD 15 CC - Project 01.zip" file is 2.45 GB in size and should take roughly 15 minutes to download to your computer using a standard broadband connection.

2   Download the second part of the lesson files by navigating to
     www.blackmagicdesign.com/dvres/grading-with-resolve15-pt2.

     The "BMD 15 CC - Project 02.zip" file is 1.01 GB in size and should take roughly five minutes to download to your computer using a standard broadband connection.

3   Download the third part of the lesson files by navigating to
     www.blackmagicdesign.com/dvres/grading-with-resolve15-pt3.

     The "BMD 15 CC - Project 03.zip" file is 2.04 GB in size and should take roughly 10 minutes to download to your computer using a standard broadband connection.

4   After downloading the zip files to your computer, open your Downloads folder, and double-click both zip files to unzip them (if your computer doesn't unzip the file automatically).

5   In your Documents folder, create a new folder called "BMD 15 - Advanced Color Correction".

6   From your Download folder, drag the "BMD 15 CC - Project 01", "BMD 15 CC - Project 02" and "BMD 15 CC - Project 03" folders into the Documents > "BMD 15 - Advanced Color Correction" folder.

You are now ready to begin Lesson 1, "Balancing Footage."

The Blackmagic Design Learning Series

Blackmagic Design publishes several official certification books as part of the Blackmagic Design Learning Series. They include:

- The Definitive Guide to DaVinci Resolve 15
- Advanced Editing with DaVinci Resolve 15
- Color Correction with DaVinci Resolve 15
- Fusion Visual Effects with DaVinci Resolve 15
- Introduction to Fairlight Audio Post with DaVinci Resolve 15
- And more to come

Whether you want to learn more advanced editing techniques, color grading, or visual effects, certified training has a learning path for you.

After completing this book, you are encouraged to take a one-hour, 50-question online proficiency exam to receive a certificate of completion from Blackmagic Design. The link to this exam is located at the end of this book.

For more information on additional books in this series and Blackmagic Design certification training, visit www.blackmagicdesign.com/products/davinciresolve/training.

Getting Certified

After completing this book, you are encouraged to take the one-hour, 50-question online proficiency exam to receive a Certificate of Completion from Blackmagic Design. The link to this exam is located at the end of this book.

When you pass the Color Correction Certified Exam, you will receive a certificate as a Certified BMD Colorist.

You'll be listed on the Blackmagic Design website and receive a Certified logo that you can proudly display on your professional website, social network page, or in your demo reel.

"No matter how much post experience you have, there's always something new to learn about DaVinci Resolve. I sometimes find that going back and reviewing the basics helps give you perspective on finding a new way to give clients the look they want quickly and efficiently. Highly recommended for newcomers and veteran colorists alike."

Marc Wielage, Senior Colorist - Chroma | Hollywood

Acknowledgments

With deepest gratitude to Patty Montesion and Dion Scoppettuolo for their mentorship and support during the writing process.

Special thanks and acknowledgements to Marc Wielage, David Hover, and Ollie Kenchington for their invaluable feedback during the test sessions of this training guide.

And extra super special thanks to editor Bob Lindstrom for his attention to detail, patience, and humor throughout the writing process.

Interface Review

This section contains an overview of the Color page interface to remind you of its key functions and to establish the terminology that will be used throughout the book.

Color Page Layout

The default layout of the Color page contains the following panels:

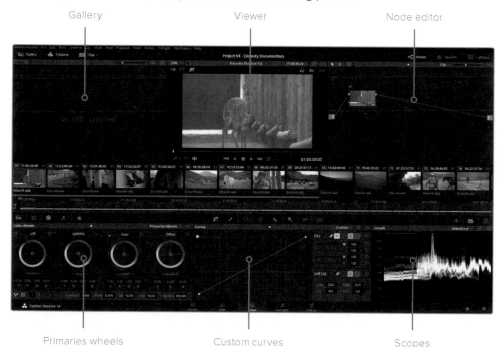

Gallery   Viewer   Node editor

Primaries wheels   Custom curves   Scopes

Gallery - contains stills which can be used for visual comparison, or for copying grading data. Stills can be generated in Resolve, or imported from an external source, and organized into albums.

Viewer - displays and plays back the selected clip, and offers additional interface controls.

Node graph - allows grades and effects to be structured in order to maximize the visual quality of each clip.

Primaries wheels - controls the tonal and chromatic values of the image on the basis of three luminance ranges (highlights, midtones and shadows).

Custom curves - gives precise control over the chromatic values of the image based on RGB and luminance curves.

Scopes - provide graphic readouts of the luminance and chrominance values of the image for the purposes of balancing and matching.

There are a series of buttons the top of the interface that allow you to show and hide panels as needed. Hiding panels (for example, the timelines or the gallery) will create more space for the viewer and remaining panels.

Primaries Wheels

The Primaries wheels (and the corresponding bars and Log wheels) of the Color wheel palette, allow you to affect the brightness and hue of the image by targeting specific luminance ranges.

Lift - targets the shadows of the image.

Gamma - targets the midtones of the image.

Gain - targets the highlights of the image.

Offset - affects the entire image uniformly.

Master wheels - the dark horizontal sliders beneath the Color wheel which control the YRGB values of those respective ranges.

Clicking the Reset arrows in the top-right corner of each wheel will neutralize the color and master wheel of that range. The entire palette can also be reset by clicking the general reset button next to the palette mode name.

The **adjustment controls** at the bottom of the Color wheel palette gives additional control over the image with features such as contrast and saturation, temp and tint, etc. Two buttons on the left allow you to switch between pages 1 and 2 of the adjustment controls.

Viewer

The viewer shows the frame that the playhead is currently on. By default, clips are represented the way they will appear upon final render. Some additional features allow you to temporarily bypass grades, see a representation of a clip's matte, and to compare clips against other media.

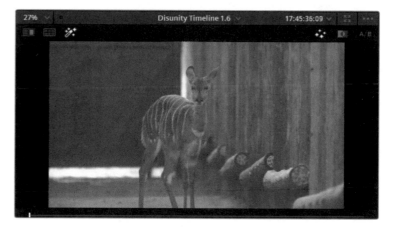

Some additional controls at the top and bottom of the viewer maximize the functionality of the tools in the Color page.

> **TIP** You can position your mouse pointer over any tool in the Color page to see its name.

Image wipe - enables you to wipe between a still, reference frame, or another clip in the timeline for visual comparison and matching.

Split screen - places clips alongside one another for review and comparison. It features several modes to allow comparison between clips on a timeline, in the same group, or even versions of grades within the same clip.

Highlight - enabling this mode will reveal the matte that is associated with a selected node.

On-screen control menu - the drop-down menu in the bottom-left of the viewer features a selection of UI controls associated with some of the palettes and functions of the Color page.

The bottom of the viewer contains a scrubber and transport controls that allow you to navigate the clip like you would in the Edit page.

Palette Panel

A series of buttons under the timeline allow you to navigate between the different palettes available on the Color page. From left to right, these palettes are:

Left palettes - Camera RAW, Color Match, Color wheel, RGB Mixer, Motion effects

Central palettes - Curves, qualifier, Window, Tracker, Blur, Key, Sizing, 3D

Keyframe editor - Scopes, Keyframe, Info

Use these buttons to navigate between palettes when prompted during the exercises. The name of each palette appears in the top-left corner when clicked, as well as over the button itself when a mouse is hovered over it.

Project File Locations and Solutions

You will find the training materials required to complete the exercises in this book divided into three project folders, which correspond to the 3 sections of the book (BMD 15 CC—Project 01, BMD 15 CC—Project 02 and BMD 15 CC—Project 03). Follow the instructions at the start of every lesson to find the necessary folder, project and timeline.

After you have completed an exercise, you have the option to review the Completed Timeline, which is included in every project file provided with the media. Keep in mind that color grading is a subjective practice and your results will often differ from the completed timelines. Rather than attempting to match your work exactly, use them for general comparison and troubleshooting.

Introduction to the Color Panels

Blackmagic Design manufactures a wide range of control surfaces for use with DaVinci Resolve 15. Professional colorists working on commercials, television, and film prefer using control surfaces over a mouse and keyboard. Hardware control surfaces allow you to work faster and more efficiently because you can adjust multiple parameters simultaneously. There are three different control panels available for Davinci Resolve: Micro, Mini and Advanced.

DaVinci Resolve
Advanced Panel

DaVinci Resolve
Micro Panel

DaVinci Resolve
Mini Panel

DaVinci Resolve Micro Panel

The DaVinci Resolve Micro Panel is a high-quality, portable, low-profile panel that features three high-resolution trackballs and 12 precision-machined control knobs for accessing essential primary correction tools. If you're using a Micro Panel, it's important to know that all of the instructions regarding the primary color tools and setup are identical to the Mini Panel. Above the center trackball are keys for switching between Log and offset color correction, as well as a key to display DaVinci Resolve's full-screen viewer, which is great for use with laptops. Eighteen dedicated keys on the right side of the panel also give you access to many commonly used grading features and playback controls. The Davinci Resolve Micro Panel is perfect for anyone that needs a truly portable solution. It's great for use on set to quickly create looks and evaluate color, it's ideal for grading in broadcast trucks, excellent for education, and ideal for anyone who's work relies mostly on the primary color correction tools.

DaVinci Resolve Mini Panel

The DaVinci Resolve Mini Panel is a compact panel that's packed with a massive combination of features and controls. As with the Advanced Panel, you get three professional trackballs along with a variety of buttons for switching tools, adding color correctors, and navigating your node tree. It also features two color LCD screens that display menus, controls, and parameter settings for the selected tool, along with buttons that give you direct access to the menus for specific features. The Mini Panel is ideal for users who regularly switch between editing and color grading, or for freelance colorists who need to carry a panel with them when moving between facilities. It's also great for colorists working on location shoots, for corporate and event videographers, for houses of worship, and more.

DaVinci Resolve Advanced Panel

For the ultimate in speed, power and control, get the DaVinci Resolve Advanced Panel! The Advanced panel has been designed in collaboration with professional colorists to work together in total harmony with the software. This large panel consists of left, center, and right consoles that give you quick, one touch access to virtually every parameter and control in the software. The DaVinci Resolve Advanced Panel lets colorists instinctively reach out and touch every part of the image, adjusting multiple parameters simultaneously with complete responsiveness for a smooth grading experience. When you're working with a client over your shoulder on a tight deadline, you need the DaVinci Resolve Advanced Panel!

Part 1: Color Correcting a DaVinci Resolve Timeline

Lessons

- Balancing footage
- Creating color continuity
- Correcting and enhancing isolated areas

Part 1 of Color Correction with DaVinci Resolve 15 focuses on establishing a strong practical foundation of primary and secondary grading techniques, with additional focus on balancing and matching media in preparation for creative grading.

Each part of this guide is accompanied by its own project, and each project is set up in a different way to reveal the variety of methods for starting a grade in Resolve. In Part 1, the project is accessed using Resolve's archiving feature.

Project File Location

You will find all the necessary content for this section in the "BMD 15 CC - Project 01" folder. Follow the instructions at the start of every lesson to find the necessary project, timeline, and media files. If you have not downloaded the first set of content files, go to the Getting Started section of this book for more information.

NOTE Although you can use DaVinci Resolve 15 for the majority of this guide, some exercises will require DaVinci Resolve 15 Studio.

Balancing Footage

The first project you will be grading is a documentary about the protection of endangered rhinos. The workflow described in the following lessons is applicable to virtually all types of video project grading, but documentary cinematography is particularly sensitive to the following steps:

- **Balance footage** - Documentary videographers often change locations during a shoot, which means they have less shot-to-shot control over lighting conditions.
- **Match shots** - Scenes, interviews and B roll can be shot over many days with different cameras. You must match this content to create a cohesive narrative.
- **Improve imagery** - You can localize grading to specific portions of a shot to enhance skies, skin tones, and visual framing.

Time

This lesson takes approximately 70 minutes to complete.

Goals

Also, you wouldn't color grade a somber documentary about rhinoceros sanctuaries as you would grade a 30-second perfume ad featuring the latest Hollywood A-lister, even if both projects were shot on the same type of camera. So, in addition to addressing the technical requirements of this footage, you will also address the documentary's aesthetic considerations.

In this lesson, you'll set up DaVinci Resolve 15 to use scene-referred color management and familiarize yourself with the primary grading tools used to balance clips on a timeline. This will be done in the context of an overall grading workflow with a purposeful approach to normalizing the footage.

Opening a Resolve Archive

This guide is divided into three distinct sections, looking at three different genres and using three different projects set up methods. The first method uses a timeline that was edited and archived in DaVinci Resolve. This is one of the most efficient methods for sharing and launching timelines, as it uses the original project file and its associated media. By restoring the DRA folder, you can be certain you are seeing the timeline exactly as intended by the editor, with all transitions, layers, and retiming intact.

Blackmagic Design Mini Panel Operations

DaVinci Resolve control panels are designed to give you fluid, hands-on control over multiple parameters at the same time, so you can work faster and be more creative. See Appendix B, "Using the Blackmagic Design Mini Panel," for an overview of how the panel can optimize your workflow in Resolve. Throughout this book, lesson notes will relate exercise workflows to actions you can perform using a Mini Panel.

NOTE For a quick refresher course on the DaVinci Resolve 15 interface, see Appendix A, "Interface Review."

1   Open DaVinci Resolve.

2   Right-click within the Project manager, and choose Restore.

3   In your hard disk, locate the BMD 15 CC - Project 1 folder.

4   In the folder, select the Project 01 - Disunity Documentary.dra file, and click Open.

5   In the Project manager, double-click the Project 01 - Disunity Documentary thumbnail
    to open the project.

6   To enter the Color page, click the Color button at the bottom of the interface,
    or press Shift-6.

7   Verify that you are on the 01 Main Timeline. The name of the timeline is written above
    the viewer. You can select the current timeline by clicking the disclosure arrow next to
    the timeline name.

> TIP You can archive projects by right-clicking a project thumbnail in the
> Project manager, and choosing Archive. Doing so will consolidate your project
> file, timelines, and media into a single folder for sharing or future retrieval.

With the project set up and the media visible in the viewer, you can now proceed with the
grading process. The next set of exercises will familiarize you with the Log-encoded color
gamuts, and how they differ from common HD (Rec.709) images.

Setting up Project Backups

As soon you create or load an existing project, it is good practice to ensure that automated
save is running in the background. These incremental backgrounds saves will keep track of
every change you make to your project, as well as retain older variants of your project for
future recall.

1   Open DaVinci Resolve > Preferences.

2   At the top of the Preferences pop-up window, switch from System to User.

3   Click "Project Save and Load" to the left to access the Save Settings.

Save Settings

✓ Live Save

By default, Live Save is enabled, so DaVinci Resolve will overwrite your active project file every time you make a change, no matter how small. This is a crucial setting to enable if you wish to minimize the risk of losing any changes to your project during unexpected system or program shutdowns.

4   Below Live Save, choose Project Backups.

Enabling this option generates a new copy of your project file at regular intervals to a designated backup location.

5   To select a backup location, click Browse, and specify a save destination on your workstation or an external drive.

By default, a backup project is generated every 10 minutes, regardless of the number of changes that you made during that period. Eventually, older project backup files are cleared from the project storage, with the exception of files that extend over longer hourly and daily intervals. This behavior can be extremely helpful when working on longform projects because it allows you to return to the state of a project from two weeks ago, for example, without sorting through thousands of project files.

6   Click Save to close the Preferences window, and return to the project. You are now safe to continue working on the project with the knowledge that your every change is being saved and backed up.

> **NOTE** To open a backed-up project file, you can access the .drp file at the designated backup location on your drive; or you can open the Project manager, right-click the thumbnail of the project you wish to restore, and choose Project Backups. In a pop-up window, you can select from a list of all the backups associated with the project.

Your project is now set up and ready for the color-grading process. However, the media in this project is currently in a Log-encoded color gamut, which does not give an accurate visual reproduction of the hues and tonal range of the recorded image. The next set of exercises will familiarize you with those Log-encoded content, and how it differs from common HD (Rec.709) images.

Maximizing the Dynamic Range

The grading potential of an image is determined primarily by its dynamic range, which is the range from its darkest point to its brightest point.

HD industrial and broadcast video cameras tend to record using a standard dynamic range based on the Rec.709 color standard. This standard ensures that images produced in the Rec.709 color space display normally on an HDTV or computer monitor. However, digital film cameras, such as the Blackmagic URSA Mini Pro, can capture a wider dynamic range by using a non-linear, or Log gamma curve. This gives you greater flexibility in manipulating the brightness, contrast, and colors without distortion.

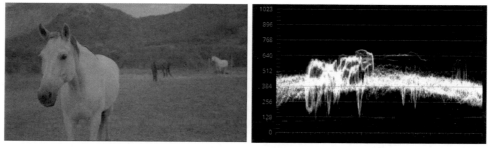

Ungraded video in log color gamut

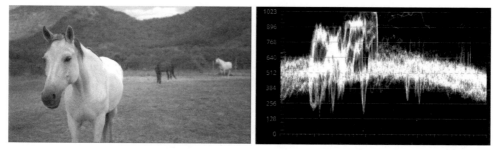

Ungraded video in rec.709 Color gamut

A by-product of encoding footage with a Log gamma curve is that footage initially appears flat and with low saturation when viewed on an HDTV or computer monitor.

By default, a colorist must first correct the Log gamma curve so that it appears correctly on the display. This process is called a *display referred* color management set up. That is, Resolve receives no direction on how the source media is meant to look, so configuring that look is left to the colorist. This process often employs look-up tables (LUTs) to convert from Log to Rec.709 (assuming HD is the final output format).

However, DaVinci Resolve also includes a scene referred color management setup that allows the colorist to assign color profiles to media based on how the media was captured. Each clip's native color gamut and gamma curve are then converted to the desired output. The colorist no longer has to manage multiple LUTs for different sources, and manually assign those LUTs to each clip.

Choosing an Input Color Space

The DaVinci YRGB color management workflow begins by enabling it in the Project settings and setting an input color space.

1   Open the Project settings by clicking the gear icon in the lower-right of the workspace.

2   Click Color Management to the left.

3   In the Color space & Transforms window, set the "Color science" menu to DaVinci YRGB Color Managed.

Below, the three color space fields are responsible for the three stages of the DaVinci YRGB color managed workflow and will define the way the color space of an image is processed and output. The Input Color space setting is based on the recording camera's gamut and gamma configuration.

4   In the Input Color space menu, choose Blackmagic Design 4.6K Film v3. This was the camera model, data level, and software version used to record most of the footage in the timeline.

5   Set the Timeline Color space and the Output Color space to Rec.709 Gamma 2.4.

The gamma of every clip in the timeline is translated from the Blackmagic Design color space to Rec.709 with the HD standard 2.4 gamma curve. The final exercise in this lesson will expand further on color gamuts and demonstrate the difference between timeline and output color spaces.

> TIP If the image in your Viewer feels too flat when completing the exercises in this lesson, change the Output Color Space to Rec.709 Gamma 2.2, which is a more appropriate gamma curve for most standard computer monitors.

6   Click Save to close the Project settings.

The colors of the clips in the timeline will shift as DaVinci YRGB color management is applied to the Color page viewer. As a result, the clips will appear more vibrant with more pronounced contrast.

DaVinci YRGB color management offers a structured, solid foundation for your primary and secondary grading stages. It does not remove the need to tweak the black point, white point, and saturation of your clips, but provides a quicker and more color-accurate way to get to a good starting point for grading.

DaVinci YRGB color management applies to all the clips in a project. If certain clips come from different sources than the rest of the timeline, you can reassign their input color spaces on an individual basis.

7   On the Color page, in 01 Main Timeline, click clips 07 and 08. These two clips come from an unknown camera source.

The project-wide color management is utilizing an input color space that does not correspond with these clips' source gamut, which is causing their colors to be incorrectly remapped and distorted. Instead of guessing the clips' origins, you can bypass the clips from being affected by color management.

8   Right-click each clip, and choose Input Color space > Bypass.

The two clips are no longer affected by the Color Science setting in the Project settings but will still be output at the same levels as the rest of the timeline.

Note how the individual input color space options in the contextual menu contained the full list of color space options in the Project settings.

The ability to assign individual input color spaces to clips can be extremely helpful when you are working on footage from multiple sources.

TIP You could use a Smart Bin to filter clip based on their sources, and then select them in batches on the timeline when changing their input color space settings.

When you don't know the Camera or Format

DaVinci YRGB color management operates at its best when you know and use the correct input data. But identifying that data can be tricky when the origins of footage are unknown, or forgotten, or data details were not included during file transfer. You can derive some useful information by examining the clip properties, but doing so will usually not provide information about the camera model or gamma range. The most definitive information can be obtained by directly contacting the production company's Project manager, director of photography, or a camera operator and requesting this information. If all else fails, you can guess at which settings appear most appropriate, or bypass DaVinci YRGB color management for specific clips and manually normalize them.

Understanding the Grading Workflow

It is good practice to have a clear idea of what your workflow is before beginning work on a project. Your workflow is informed by a variety of factors including the color space and format of your footage, the way that the timeline edit was shared with you, and the content of the project, itself. Before continuing with your project, let's review the common phases of a grading workflow.

Balancing and Shot Matching

Before you can grade footage creatively, you must adjust shot luminance and chrominance to create a level starting point for your grade. This process is akin to laying down a primer on a canvas before painting to ensure that the pigment is applied to a consistent surface.

A single grade applied to five balanced and matched shots will have continuity and flow naturally from one shot to the next; whereas the same grade applied to mismatched shots will continue to reflect each shot's differences.

This stage of grading is referred to as a *primary grade* because the entire frame of the image is adjusted. It is usually approached using techniques known as normalization, balancing, and shot matching.

Normalization and balancing, involves creating a neutral starting point for each clip in the timeline by consistently adjusting the luminance levels of each clip, and neutralizing any issues with the color balance.

Shot matching involves comparing clips to one another and matching their contrast and colors exactly. This technique is particularly advantageous when the majority of your footage already has a similar look, and you need tweak only a few exceptional shots to create a smooth starting point for your scene.

Performing Secondary Grading

Secondary grading refers to any part of the grading process in which only a part of an image is altered. The potential for secondary grading is limitless, but it is mainly achieved by two means: *keying and masking*.

Keying targets a portion of an image based on a hue, saturation, or luminance range. In Resolve, the main tool for key extraction is the qualifier.

Masking employs geometric vector shapes to isolate a portion of an image. Resolve's masking interface, the Power Windows palette, features some standard shapes (linear, circle, polygon, and gradient), as well as a fully customizable power curve that enables you to generate garbage mattes and rotoscopes (animated masks).

Like the qualifier, Power Windows cannot alter the appearance of an image directly, but act as selectors for the grading tools.

Secondary grading is at its most powerful when the qualifier and Power Windows are used in tandem. While the qualifier focuses on extracting an element with a clean edge, a power window can confine the qualifier's influence to a specific portion of the screen. In this way, it is possible to target an object in the presence of other areas of the shot that are of the same key range.

Creating a Look

Once your footage is balanced and shot matched, and any individual secondary grading needs are met, your creative process can begin.

When performing creative grading, you should carefully consider the emotional and narrative implications of the scene. You can use the primary grade to influence an audience's emotional perception of an environment by tweaking a scene's temperature to indicate positive (warm) or negative (cold) moods, as well as a wide range of additional psychological color and tone associations. Additionally, the creative grade can communicate practical narrative elements such as a change in location or time (for non-linear stories).

> **NOTE** The grading workflow described here does not rigidly dictate the order in which these grades must be performed by the colorist. Although first completing the balancing and shot matching stage is strongly advised, it is often necessary to return to and readjust the grades applied in earlier stages to ensure a consistent final output.

Visualizing the Grading Workflow in the Node Editor

The following chart represents a traditional grading workflow in the context of the Node editor in Resolve's Color page.

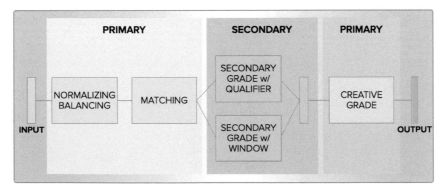

This graph is not intended as a literal guideline to how nodes should be structured, but a representative overview of how nodes relate to one another and their relative positions.

Setting Tonal Range and Contrast

The human eye is particularly sensitive to light sources and shadows, which is why it makes sense to begin the normalization and grading processes by establishing the luminance of an image.

In the following exercises, you will make luminance adjustments using master wheels and custom curves while learning about the waveform monitor.

Normalizing with Master Wheels

The Color wheel are one of the most integral primary color correction tools used to adjust the hue of an image. Beneath them, the master wheels allow you to set the tonal range and contrast of the image by targeting its luminance.

In this exercise, you will adjust the depth of the shadows and the height of the highlights with the master wheels. You'll also enable the waveform scope to monitor your adjustments for unwanted clipping.

1 Select clip 02.

The palette in the lower-right corner of the DaVinci Resolve interface is currently set to the Scopes panel in Waveform mode.

The waveform scope represents the luminance and color channel values of the video at the precise timeline position of the playhead.

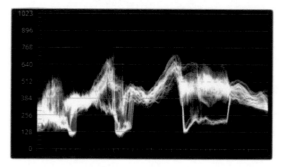

The vertical axis of the scope represents the entire luminance range of the image.

The bottom of the display represents the blackest black (0 in a 10-bit depth signal), and the top represents the whitest white (1023 in 10-bit). Everything between represents the full midtones range of the image in a greyscale format.

The horizontal axis represents the image itself and can be read from left to right (or vice versa) on both the graph and the monitor. You can think of the display as showing a redistribution of the pixels (the trace) along their respective vertical columns based on their luminance levels with darker areas of the footage placed further down the graph, and lighter areas brought to the top.

Each color channel is overlapped in the trace. White in the trace indicates that each channel has an equal amount of intensity. When adjusting tonality in an image, you can disable the RGB channels in the waveform and show only luminance.

2   In the upper-right corner of the waveform, click the settings button.

3   Click the Y channel button to view only the luminance channel.

4   Click anywhere in Resolve to close the waveform settings window.

Any part of the trace that goes below 0 (black point) and above 1023 (white point) in the sRGB gamut will be clipped, which will result in a loss of detail in the image.

A good starting point when first normalizing footage is to ensure that the shadows are floating at around 5-10% above the black point (0) on the scope, while the pure white highlights (if any) safely stop well under the white point (90%), leaving the remaining 10% for superwhite elements – such as blown out headlights, lens flares, or metallic specular highlights – which can extend beyond the white point.

5   In the Color page, open the Color wheel palette.

If you have already used DaVinci Resolve, or if you have read through Appendix A, "Interface Review," you will know that, the Lift wheel will affect the image shadows, the Gamma wheel will affect the midtones, and the Gain will affect the highlights. The Offset wheel impacts the entire image and can be thought of as a combination of all three wheels.

The horizontal wheels located under the Color wheel are called master wheels, and impact the luminance values of those ranges.

6   Drag the Lift master wheel to the left to darken the shadows. Because this image has detail in the darkest areas of the wood, aim for the lowest parts of the waveform trace to fall far above 0 but below the 128 line.

Notice the three areas of the graph where the trace of the waveform dips toward the black level. Try to locate their respective positions in the frame.

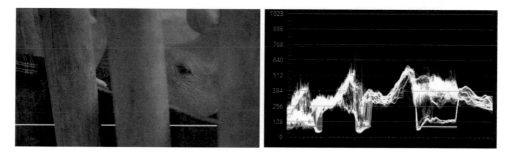

Those three dark areas correspond to the places where the barrier is visible behind the wooden poles in the enclosure. The darkest parts of the barrier are represented by a pronounced dip in the graph.

7   You can use the Gain master wheel to brighten the lighter areas of the image. The image has no chart or reference for pure white, but you could use the thumb in the image as an indicator for luminance. The highlights of light skin tones should rest between 50-75% on the waveform graph. Drag the Gain master wheel so the tallest parts of trace does not go higher than 3/4 on the waveform graph.

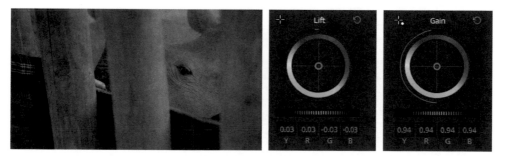

This is an example of using image context for balancing and grade adjustment. In future exercises, you will continue to keep an eye on elements which you can use as a guide for grading decisions.

With the shadow and highlight levels set, you will want to adjust the brightness of the midtones.

8   Drag the Gamma master wheel to the right to lighten the overall scene and enhance the details of the rhino's wrinkled skin.

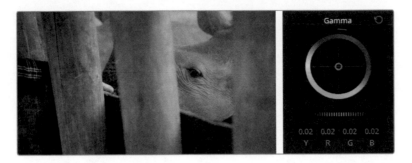

After setting the tonal range, you will further enhance the image details. The master wheels affect the luminance too broadly at this stage, so you should use the contrast control to refine the distinction between the darker and lighter areas.

9   At the bottom of the Color wheel palette, in the adjustment controls, drag the contrast setting to the right to increase the level of detail in the skin and the wooden poles.

Your image will start look a little dark, but that's OK. So far you have been focusing on only the depth of the shadows, and the nature of the contrast.

10 To increase brightness, but maintain the shadows and level of contrast, drag the pivot control next to the contrast.

The pivot control establishes the balance of the contrast by placing more or less priority to either side of the luminance scale. By lifting it, you will increase the overall brightness and clarity of the image This will come at the inverse expense of the shadows, which will be reduced.

11 Press Cmd-D (macOS) or Ctrl-D (Windows), to toggle the bypass on and off. Compare your before and after results to evaluate how altering the contrast has affected the image. Tweak the values if the grade becomes overpowering.

Bypassed

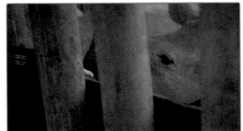

Graded

The grading process usually requires a lot of back-and-forth tweaking of palette values while monitoring the waveform. Some changes dramatically offset the effects of prior adjustments, as in this example, when increasing the contrast darkened the shadows, which prompted additional tweaks. Iteration is a completely natural part of the grading process.

Using the Mini Panel - offset mode

Whereas the DaVinci Resolve 15 interface shows four wheels within the primary tool palette (Lift, Gamma, Gain, and Offset), you'll notice that the hardware-based Mini Panel has three wheels and trackballs. To access the Offset tool, press the Offset button directly above the Gamma wheel. When the Offset button is illuminated (we'll call it Offset mode), the Gain wheel and trackball will control the master Offset. Just as when adjusting Lift, Gamma, or Gain, moving the wheel will control brightness while the trackball controls color.

Additionally, when in Offset mode, your Lift and Gamma wheels control Temperature and Tint, respectively. To exit Offset mode, press the illuminated Offset button once again. When it no longer lights up, your trackballs and wheels will return to controlling Lift, Gamma, and Gain.

Setting Contrast with more Flexibility

Curves are another major grading tool used for both primary and secondary adjustments. Whereas the master wheels target the luminance range of an image, the curves affect the image based on its luminance or RGB color channels.

The curves controls allow you to manipulate the image with great precision and flexibility.

1   In the timeline, click clip 03.

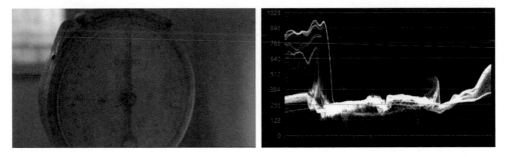

Because the colors in the image are flat, the majority of the waveform graph is condensed in the lower midtones. A significant elevation appears to the left, where a window is positioned behind the scale; and to the right is a gentle peak where the light reflects off the plastic rim.

2   Choose Workspace > Viewer Mode > Enhanced Viewer, or press Option-F (macOS) or Alt-F (Windows), to enlarge the viewer.

The Clips timeline and surrounding palettes collapse, dynamically enlarging the size of the viewer. The image becomes much easier to see for grading work.

3   Ensure that the custom curve palette is active in the central palettes of the Color page.

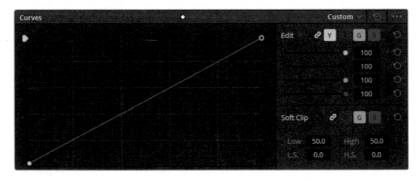

The lower-left of the curve graph represents the darkest potential point of the image, and the upper-right represents the whitest.

The horizontal axis represents the luminance range of the image itself, while the vertical represents the offset of that luminance range. By raising or lowering the two control points at either extreme of the curve, you can manipulate the distribution of the tonal range.

By default, the luminance curve (Y) will be visible for adjustment, ganged to all three color channels (R, G, B).

4   Click the Y channel button to ungang the channels.

Now, instead of adjusting RGB values you are only manipulating the luminance of the image.

5   Drag the lowest control point on the luminance curve across the floor to the right.

Doing so lowers the waveform of the image logarithmically, darkening it in the shadows faster than in the highlights.

6   Stop dragging the control point when the bottom of the trace is still above the 0 line of the waveform.

You can add more control points to the curve to manipulate the midtones of the image. Let's tackle the lower midtones that appear too dark after the black point adjustment.

7   Click the lower half of the curve to create a new control point that will target the lower midtones.

> **TIP** Shift-click when creating a control point to prevent the curve from moving at the position of the mouse.

8   Drag the control point up to raise the lower midtones and brighten up the face of the scale.

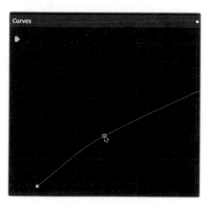

9   Create another control point in the upper midtones, and drag it down to prevent the window from getting too bright.

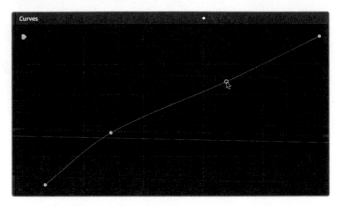

Many colorists prefer setting the tonal range and contrast in the custom curves because it offers much finer control over the contrast amount, the pivot point, and the intensity of each luminance level of the image.

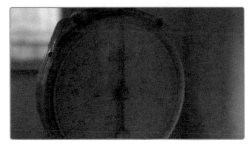

Bypassed

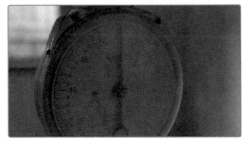

Graded

Balancing Colors

After adjusting the tonal range and contrast of an image, you begin to carefully examine the colors and neutralize them in preparation for grading. An unbalanced image will affect the precision of your grade, the quality of any keyed elements, and will stand out in a sequence of balanced clips.

Balancing Color with Curves

You can use custom curves to manipulate the three color channels with great tractability by creating dedicated control points for each segment of the luminance on each channel.

1   Click the waveform setting button and disable the Y channel button to view the RGB channels.

When balancing an image using the waveform, all three channels making the trace appear white when the channels are aligned. In an image that should have white highlights, the trace will appear white at the top.

2   Review clip 03 alongside the waveform.

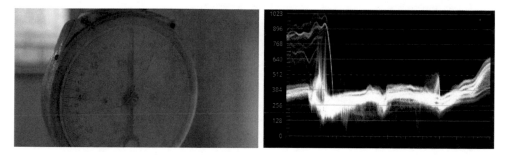

The red channel appears elevated above the other channels, which is giving the image a slightly warm tint, especially in the window.

3   In the custom curves palette, Click the red (R) button to select the red channel.

4   Click the top of the red curve and drag it downward. Pay attention to the waveform and drag until the red highlight overlaps the blue and green channels in the trace, resulting in white along the upper edge of the graph.

5   Create a second point on the red curve to perform the same action in the midtones. Drag until the lower half of the trace appears white.

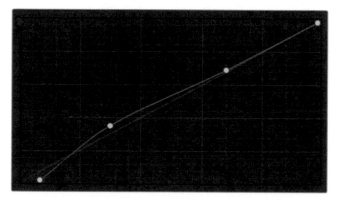

Though the red is corrected, the image now has a mild yellow tint because the blue channel has less presence in the highlights and midtones.

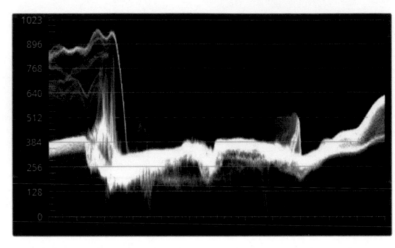

6   Click B to isolate the blue channel, and drag the upper point of the blue curve left across the top of the curve interface until the waveform appears more neutral.

7   Click the center of the blue curve line to add a control point, and drag it up until the midtones in the waveform are aligned.

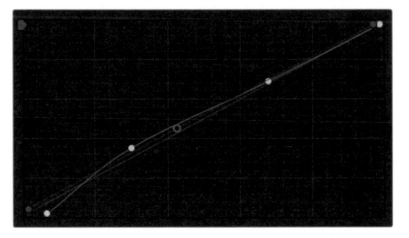

8   Press Cmd-D (macOS) or Ctrl-D (Windows) to disable color adjustments, then press that keyboard shortcut again to see the corrected image.

With the luminance of the overall image altered, you could opt to return to the Y curve and further adjust the tonal range and contrast of the image, if necessary.

Using the Mini Panel - Curves

You can use the Mini Panel to control all of your curves in DaVinci Resolve. If you used your keyboard and mouse in DaVinci Resolve, or any other image-processing application, chances are you've already worked with curves. While you might be used to controlling curves using a mouse, the Mini Panel places dozens of preset curve points at your disposal. You'll can enter Curves mode by pressing the Curves button in the upper-left area of the Mini Panel.

If you've already selected a specific curve tool with your mouse, the Mini Panel will jump to that tool. Otherwise, the default curves that the Mini Panel will jump to are your Custom Curves.

The curve tools provide an excellent way to explore the diversity and functionality of your Mini Panel. Every major type of curve featured in Resolve may be activated by the soft buttons on the top of the five-inch screens. The knobs allow you to control specific points of the curve that is currently activated. For custom curves, intervals of 0%, 20%, 40%, 60%, 80%, and 100% may be adjusted. This functionality allows you to control more than one curve point at a time, which will save time, help develop muscle memory, and allow you to make more creative color grading decisions.

Understanding Log Controls and Primaries Wheels

Before you proceed normalizing the next clip, it is worthwhile taking a slight detour to understand another function that can be a fundamental part of primary grading and balancing: The Log Color wheel.

It is easier to grasp the difference between the Primaries wheels and the Log controls by first observing a graphic example before moving on to image adjustment. Let's use the simple gradient image at the end of the timeline and manipulate its brightness to compare how the two adjustments affect it.

1   Choose Workspace > Viewer Mode > Enhanced Viewer, or press Option-F (macOS) or Alt-F (Windows), to see the timeline clips.

2   Select the last clip in the timeline (the grayscale image).

In the standard Primaries wheels that you are familiar with, the Lift, Gamma, and Gain wheels target the luminance ranges as seen in the following figure:

A wide overlap occurs between the segments. When you try to manipulate the shadows of the image using the Lift color or master wheels, the change also substantially affects the midtones, and even the brighter ranges of the image.

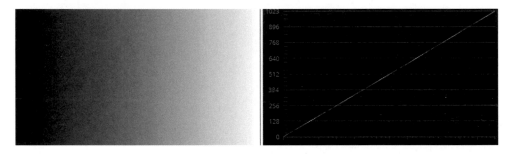

NOTE To see a linear gradient and waveform as you perform this exercise, in Coloir Management, set the Color Science to DaVinci YRGB. Remember to return Color Science to DaVinci YRGB Color Managed before continuing to the next lesson.

The waveform scope displays the gradient clip as a perfect diagonal line travelling left to right from 0 to 1023, thereby representing its linear transition from black to white in the image.

3   Drag the Gain master wheel to the left to darken the upper ranges of the gradient.

In the waveform, the bottom of the diagonal line remains connected to the black point. The brightest part of the gradient is affected most severely, but still exerts substantial impact on the rest of the luminance range.

4   Reset the Gain master wheel.

5   Drag the Lift master wheel to the right to brighten the lower ranges of the gradient.

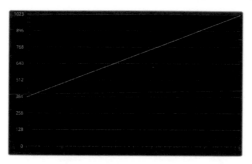

Opposite to the Gain wheel, the majority of the Lift wheel impact is on the darkest portion of the gradient with the effect tapering off linearly as it reaches the top of the waveform.

The main point is that in both the gain and lift adjustments, the entire image, except the white and black points, are changed. This is intentional because this wide overlap creates nice, smooth transitions even with dramatic changes.

6   Reset the Lift master wheel.

When working in Log, the luminance ranges are much more distinctly defined:

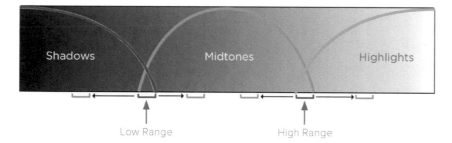

Manipulating the image shadows will have very little effect on the rest of the luminance range due to the small amount of overlap between the shadows and the midtones range.

7   In the options menu in the Color wheel palette, choose Log.

On the surface, this interface looks identical to the Primaries wheels. However, adjustments to the shadows, midtones, and highlights react very differently.

8 Drag the Highlight master wheel to the left to darken the highlights of the gradient.

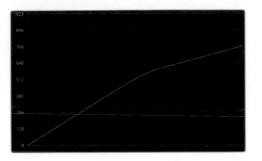

The upper-third of the waveform bends until it is horizontal, but has no impact on the shadows. This behavior is reflected in the viewer, in which the brightest portion of the gradient are darkened, but the midtone and shadows remain the same.

9 Drag the Shadow master wheel to the right to brighten the dark ranges.

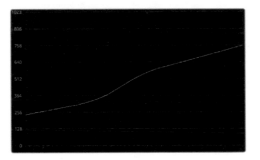

This time, the lower-third of the line rises until it is parallel to the horizon.

With the waveform in this position, it is easy to see how you can affect the position of overlap between the shadows and midtones (low range), and the midtones and highlights (high range).

10 In the adjustment settings under the Log wheels, drag the LR value to the left to move the low range farther down toward the shadows, giving priority to the midtones controls.

11 Drag the HR value to the right to move the high range toward the shadows for the same effect, but in reverse.

TIP To further appreciate how primaries and Log differ, drag the color indicator inside the Lift and Shadow wheels to see how the gradient is affected. Adjusting the Lift wheel will cause the entire gradient to change hue, whereas dragging the Shadow wheel will constrain the color change to the darkest edge of the gradient.

The Primaries wheels can be extremely useful when you are attempting to change the luminance or chrominance of a narrower image luminance range. The next exercise will demonstrate a practical use of switching between primaries and Log wheels.

Applying Log and Primaries Changes to an Image

With an understanding of how you can target the luminance ranges of an image, you can now adjust the tonal range and balance of an image with more accuracy.

1 Select clip 07, and switch the waveform to view the Y luminance channel.

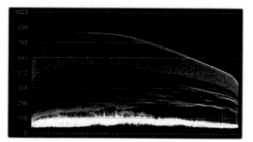

The luma waveform indicates some room for adjustment of the image's highlights and shadows. However, before proceeding with the tonal adjustment, let's check the Parade scope to determine the presence of color in the luminance ranges.

2 Switch the scopes panel to Parade.

Waveform

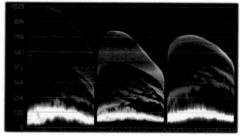

Parade

The Parades show sufficient luminance in the red channel. Increasing the brightness of the image will have the effect of blowing out the sky.

With reliable white and black references in an image, standard procedure is to neutralize the three channels to achieve harmony. Without references, context is important. In this case, the context is the sunset with its accompanying red skyline, which requires an exception to the balancing rule.

3   Switch the scopes back to Waveform. With the highlights analyzed, you can focus on the tonal range and balance of the dark foreground elements.

4   To increase the overall brightness of the image without clipping the highlights, drag the Gamma master wheel slightly to the right.

The image shadows appear to be compressed along a narrow luminance range which is causing lose of the detail in the image foreground. Adjusting the Lift master wheel would only increase the darkness and suppress more of the details.

5   Drag the Lift master wheel left to see how dramatically it affects the foreground. The entire image becomes too dark with even the smallest adjustment.

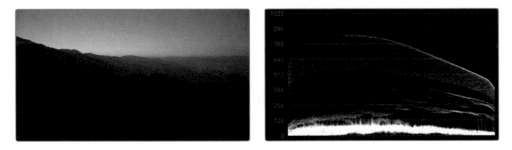

6   Reset the Lift wheel.

7   Switch the Color wheel palette to Log.

> TIP Press Option-Z (macOS) or Alt-Z (Windows) to toggle between the primaries and Log wheels.

8   Drag the Shadow master wheel to the left to lower the black point without clipping it. Note that the tree details begin to pop out against the mountains and ground.

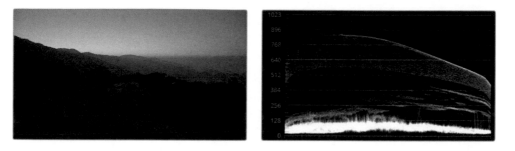

Because the Shadow wheel is more dedicated to the lower ranges of luminance, it is not affecting the midtones as dramatically as the Lift wheel was. With the contrast adjusted, you can now address the colors. This is a particularly tricky image because of the conditions under which it was captured. The sun is still rising, which is resulting in beautiful peach, purple, and blue hues to graduate throughout the sky. You will strive retain these unusual hues in the sky, while normalizing the colors in the ground – most notably, the magenta in the shadows.

9 Click the color indicator in the Shadow wheel, and drag it gently away from the magenta side of the wheel toward green. Stop dragging before the green in the shadows becomes too overpowering.

Before shadow grade

After shadow grade

This adjustment removes the magenta tint from the shadows and lower midtones of the image while preserving the hues in the mountains and the sky.

10 If necessary, return to the Log wheels and further refine the shadows by dragging the master wheel and adjusting the color wheel indicator.

As demonstrated in this exercise, primaries and Log wheels can be used very effectively together. Whereas you can use the primaries as a means of establishing tonal range and contrast, Log wheels behave like a secondary adjustment that can further refine the three luminance ranges.

Log wheels are particularly effective for working on under or overexposed footage. They allow for restorative work in the high and lower ranges, as well as minor tweaks to the brightness and hue of those ranges without seriously affecting the remainder of the image.

Together with balancing and matching, they are also powerful tools for creating distinct creative looks.

Exploring a Color Managed Workflow

At the start of this lesson, you looked at a few settings in DaVinci YRGB color management. One of the most powerful aspects of using a color-managed workflow in DaVinci Resolve is that you can change the output color space at any time based on your final delivery requirements.

Doing so is particularly helpful when you need to output multiple masters to different destinations. You may want one master for Rec.709 HD, another for Rec.2020 UHD, and yet another for P3 digital cinema. Resolve maintains of your color decisions and manages the color transformations without you needing to change a thing on the Color page.

1   Open Project settings > Color Management.

2   Set the Output Color space menu to the Rec.2020 Gamma 2.4.

3   Click Save to save the new output color space settings.

The color space is changed, and the viewer reflects the updated results. If you had a calibrated UHD Rec.2020 display you would notice that the grading you applied to your clips in Rec.709 HD is retained and displayed correctly.

Accurate Color Monitoring in DaVinci Resolve

Resolve was designed to work with industry-standard calibrated external displays connected via video output interfaces to enable critical color evaluation.

Most computer monitors are incapable of displaying the color gamut or gamma range required for broadcast and theatrical distribution. Additionally, most computer displays have their own color and contrast calibration as determined by the manufacturer, which is further altered by the workstation's operating system. For this reason, their color accuracy cannot be fully guaranteed to carry across after delivery, even when moving between different video players on the same machine.

Ideally, you should use an external monitor and video interface for all grading work. Alternatively, you could use a color calibration probe to analyze your computer display and generate a LUT that will remap the colors to the correct standard.

4   Open Project settings > Color Management.

5   Set the Output Color space menu back to the default Rec.709 Gamma 2.4.

6   Click Save to save the new output color space settings.

> **TIP** When using the Rec.709 color space, the general rule is to use 2.2 gamma when preparing work for web content, and to use 2.4 when preparing to output for broadcast or theatrical screening.
>
> Revert the color space back to Log when sending materials to VFX compositors. Your color corrections will be retained in the image and visible to the VFX artists when they color manage the media on their end.

You can also change the gamma range separately from the color space by selecting the "Use Separate Color space and Gamma" checkbox above the color space menus.

Separating the color space and gamma settings allows you to have full control over the chrominance and luminance processing of your footage. You can indicate gamma ranges that are not part of the standard preset selection of the color space menus.

Choosing the Timeline Color Space

When utilizing color management, the Input Color Space of the video signal is first remapped to the Timeline Color Space, which impacts the processing of the signal on a timeline level and impacts the behaviour of the grading tools.

The resulting signal is then remapped to the Output Color Space, which affects its final appearance in the Viewer. This dual treatment of the signal allows you to continue grading a project with the same grading tools, even when switching between different output standards.

In this exercise, you will compare how the grading controls are affected under different timeline color spaces.

> **easyDCP Delivery**
>
> When grading with the intention of exporting to the easyDCP format, your choice of timeline color space will determine the color management of the DCP, whether you have color management enabled or not.
>
> Set the timeline color space to Rec.709 Gamma 2.4 to render the DCP with the correct Rec.709 to XYZ matrix.

1   In the main timeline, click clip 01. It is currently color managed to output in the Rec.709 color space at a Gamma 2.4 range.

First, you will check how the change in the timeline color space will affect an ungraded clip.

2   Open the Project settings, and in Color Management, set the Timeline Color space to Rec.709 (Scene).

Rec.709 (Scene) refers to a distribution of the gamma curve meant to emulate the physical behaviour of cathode ray tube (CRT) displays. It is mostly obsolete in the context of modern HDTV. In this exercise it is being used for demonstrative purposes.

3   Click Save to confirm the change.

This change did not impact the image in the viewer because the project's output color space remained unchanged (Rec.709 with Gamma 2.4), and also because the clip is not currently graded. The Timeline Color space setting will affect only how the grading tools perform their function.

4   In the custom curves, click Y to isolate the luma channel.

5   Drag the Y channel white down until it reaches the first bold horizontal line in the graph.

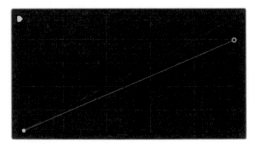

The image will become darker, most notably in the brighter areas.

6 Right-click in the viewer, and grab a still of the grade.

7 Double click under the still thumbnail and enter the label **Rec Scene TCS**.

8 Reset the custom curve.

9 Return to the Project settings, and reset the Timeline Color space to Rec.709 Gamma 2.4.

Now with the timeline color space changed, you'll perform the same adjustment.

10 In the custom curves palette, drag down the anchor at the top of the curve until it reaches the first bold horizontal line in the graph.

11 Double-click the Rec.Scene Timeline CS still in the gallery to compare it side-by-side in the viewer with the same adjustment done in a Gamma 2.4 timeline color space.

TIP You can switch from a horizontal to a vertical wipe using the buttons in the upper-right corner of the viewer, or right-clicking and choosing Wipe Style > Vertical.

Comparing the two shots shows a uniform shift in the brightness of the image. Though the output color space has remained the same, the standard at which the grading palettes are operating changed.

For this reason, it is highly advisable not to change your timeline color space after grading begins. Doing so could have a significant impact on the appearance of the luminance and colors in graded clips, which you can only change manually or by resetting the timeline color space to its initial standard.

12 Click the Image wipe button in the upper-left corner of the viewer to turn off the wipe mode.

It is important to recognise that the Timeline Color Space setting defines the color gamut and dynamic range at the starting point of the grade. If you choose a narrow gamut/range in the Timeline Color Space, you will be unable to expand it to a wider standard in the Output Color Space without experiencing degradation of the video signal. For example, let's say you were starting work on a project that needed to be delivered in both HDR and HD standards. The correct workflow would be to set both the Timeline and Output Color Spaces to an HDR gamut and dynamic range (e.g. Rec.2020) at the very start. After completing the grade, you would then switch the Output Color Space to HD (Rec.709).

If uncertain, your safest option is to set your timeline color space to match your output color space.

Self-guided Exercises #1

Complete the following exercises in the 01 Main Timeline to test your understanding of the tools and workflows covered in this lesson.

Clip 01 - Continue to balance this clip using the custom curves controls. Place additional controls points in the low and high midtones to create a contrast and accentuate the details in the wood grain.

Clip 02 - Use the Contrast and Pivot controls to enhance the details on the scale.

Clip 04, 05, 06, and 09 - Use the Primaries wheels to establish a tonal range and contrast on these clips with the assistance of the waveform scope.

Clip 12, 16, and 17 - Using custom curves, and with the Parade scope for reference, normalize these clips and balance the colors as necessary.

When you've completed these exercises, open the 04 Completed Timeline to compare your balancing to the Balance node in this "solved" timeline. Note that normalization, balancing, and contrast in most of the clips was separated into individual actions in the Node editor. In the next lesson, you will also begin the practice of separating your grading stages into nodes.

Lesson Review

1   Does a DaVinci Resolve archive (.DRA) contain the original project media?

2   What does the Y in YRGB represent?

3   What does the Pivot in the adjustment controls do?

4   What is the difference between the Primary Wheels and Log controls?

5   Where do you enable DaVinci YRGB Color Management settings?

Answers

1   Yes. Archived projects (.DRA) consolidate all related project media within a single folder that can be restored through the Project Manager.

2   The Y refers to luminance.

3   Adjusts contrast balance.

4   They target different tonal ranges of the image.

5   Project Settings > Color Management.

Creating Color Continuity

When editing footage for a video project, the end goal often is to create a single running narrative that appears to be happening in real time. Much of the time – even in documentary filmmaking – this unity of time is an illusion. Materials for a single scene can take days or even weeks to photograph which can result in fluctuations in light, temperature, and tint as environmental factors influence the footage from one day to the next.

The goal of shot matching is to assess how multiple clips compare to one another when placed into a timeline, and to ensure that they create color continuity. When shots don't match, an audience becomes aware of their artificial sequencing (as opposed to actual events shot in real time), which breaks the illusion of cinema and compromises the viewers suspension of disbelief.

In the previous lesson, you looked at the most common tools and workflows for shot balancing, and cleaned up the contrast and color cast of shots in preparation for a grade. In this lesson, you'll examine the shot matching process.

Time

This lesson takes approximately 60 minutes to complete.

Goals

Building a Shot-matching Strategy

Your approach to shot matching will depend greatly upon the nature of the footage.

On a narrative production shot by an experienced cinematographer and camera crew the quality of the raw content can have a reliable consistency throughout and require a minimal normalization effort.

For documentaries, the fluctuation in locations, light sources, and temperatures (not to mention content shot on different cameras) may require a much more dedicated preparation stage.

It is normal to incorporate both balancing and shot matching during the first primary grade pass, however the two should be treated as separate jobs and it is highly advisable to keep them on separate nodes.

Your shot-matching strategy could be narrowed down to the following approaches and considerations:

- **Balance all shots in a sequence**. This workflow assumes a shot-by-shot approach to normalizing the luminance range and balancing of every shot in the sequence, which will result in a uniform sequence of shots. This is a time-consuming method which is best reserved for projects with vastly mismatched media sources or lighting conditions (archival documentaries, promo videos, etc).

Every clip balanced individually

- **Adjust only mismatched shots in a sequence**. If only one or two shots in a sequence have a contrasting color balance, it makes sense to adjust only them to create an even starting point for the grade. This approach is more common to standard grading practices.

Mismatched clips graded to match rest of sequence

- **Select a master reference shot**. Sometimes you will have more than one clip that could be used as a reference for matching. In those cases, either opt for the reference that will have a less extreme impact on the color spaces of the other clips.

Clips adjusted to key shot that causes least color distortion

Or consider settling on the clip that is closest in appearance to your intended grade. That done, any further creative grading will aim to enhance the colors, not undo them.

Clips adjusted to key shot that is closer to final intended look

TIP When selecting a master reference shot, it is best to select a wide angle of the scene and match all other angles to it. A wide angle shot is likely to have the best overall representation of the light sources, temperatures and tones, as well as most of the physical elements in the scene. In contrast, a close-up might contain less reliable data for balancing and share few elements with other shots.

The exercises in the following lessons will focus on the practical implementation of matching based on these methods. Understanding the variety of matching methods that are available in DaVinci Resolve 15 will enable you to construct grading workflows that are best suited to your coloring abilities and project type.

Organizing Shots Using Flags and Filters

In the previous lesson, you were clicking on various clips throughout the timeline. Resolve provides helpful organizational tools called flags that can assist in identifying and categorizing clips based on any criteria that you define. For example, you might flag clips with overexposed skies along with objects that need color hue adjustments; or flag clips that require green screen keying, or narrative-specific dynamic grades.

1   In the timeline menu above the viewer, open the 02 Balanced Timeline.

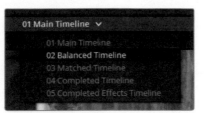

The timelines in this project already have some flags set. You'll add a few more to identify the clips you will need for the matching exercises in this lesson.

2 In the timeline, right-click clip 04, and choose Flags > Green.

A green flag appears in the upper-left corner of the clip thumbnail to indicate that the clip is flagged.

Another method for applying flags is to use a keyboard shortcut.

3 Click clip 05. Press G on your keyboard to add another flag.

While this is a faster technique for applying flags, it has applied the wrong color flag.

4 To change the flag to green, double-click the blue flag on the thumbnail to open the Flags dialog.

Note that the dialog window allows you to attach notes to flag, which is very handy for future grading reference.

5 Select the green-colored flag, and click Done to close the dialog.

The keyboard shortcut currently is configured to apply blue flags by default. To change the default flag color, you will need to change the flag color in the toolbar of the Edit page.

6   Go to the Edit page. Next to the Flag icon in the toolbar, click the drop disclosure arrow, and choose Yellow.

7   Switch back to the Color page, select clips 04 and 06, and press G to apply yellow flags to them.

TIP You can apply a flag to multiple clips by selecting a range of thumbnails, and then using any of the methods in this exercise to apply the desired flag to the selected clips.

The green flags in the timeline identify the clips you will be working on throughout this lesson. It will be easier to locate and navigate between them if you filter the timeline to show only the green-flagged clips.

8   At the top of the Color page, click the disclosure arrow next to the Clips button, andchoose Flagged Clips > Green Flag.

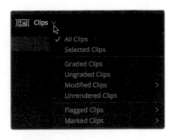

> **TIP** When a filter is applied to a timeline, the Clips button is underlined in red to serve as a visual reminder that some clips in the timeline might not be visible to you due to the filter.

You have temporarily hidden all clips that do not have a green flag applied to them. The result is a significantly simplified timeline that will help you focus on the flagged clips without the need to navigate around your timeline to locate them.

> **TIP** Like flags, you can also use markers for filtering purposes. The difference is that flags identify an entire clip (or source media), whereas markers single out a specific frame or range on a clip in the timeline. Adding a flag to a clip adds it to every instance that the source clip appears in a timeline. Markers can be applied using a keyboard shortcut (M) and their default color may be set in the toolbar of the Edit page.

9   Once again, click the disclosure arrow next to the Clips button, and choose Flagged Clips > Yellow Flag.

As you can see, clips are capable of containing multiple flags. This means that media classifications can overlap, which will allow you to filter clips that have several workflow roles.

10   Enter the Clips pop-up menu, and choose Yellow again to remove yellow flags from the clip filter.

In Resolve, flags and filters can perform a wide variety of functions. You could use different flag colors to identify clips that must be reframed due to a visible boom, single out clips that were incorrectly white balanced, or isolate clips that require a flashback look. When the timeline is filtered based on flag color, you can focus on addressing just one category of clips at a time.

Applying Shot Match

The shot match function in Resolve analyzes the colors in one image and reconfigures the balance of another image (or multiple images) to match it.

The results of any algorithmic grading function should be taken with a pinch of salt because the algorithm is unable to recognize environmental factors behind the colors of a scene. Regardless, using shot match can be a great starting point for a match grade, and could enable the colorist to quickly prepare shots for on-set review, or dailies processing.

1   In the green flag-filtered timeline, select clip 01.

You will be matching the colors in this clip to the balanced clip 02 directly after it. In the interest of preserving the integrity of the video signal, you are advised to keep normalization, balancing, and matching on separate nodes.

2   Press Option-S (macOS) or Alt-S (Windows) to add a third node on clip 01.

3   Right-click the second node, and choose Change Label. Name the node **Shot Match**.

NOTE In the Balanced Timeline, the normalization and balancing stages were organized into dedicated nodes. This method represents a common grading workflow that focuses on preserving the integrity of the RGB signal. You will explore it in greater depth in Part 2 of this book.

4   Right-click clip 02, and choose "Shot Match to This Clip". The shot match is performed on the active clip in the timeline, which is currently clip 01.

The result is a good match between the two images. Clip 01 is made warmer and less contrasted to match the environment in clip 02.

Before match

After match

Automatic shot matching can be great for quickly realizing an approximation of a match, to create a starting point for manual match grade, or to provide quick demonstrations to clients. But ultimately, you should still assess the image visually and check its video scopes to confirm an accurate match. If necessary, perform manual adjustments to the grading tools to refine the match.

Matching Shots Using Stills

Stills have a variety of functions in Resolve, as will be explored in lessons throughout the book. One of the most direct uses of stills is for visually comparing clips in the viewer. By superimposing a snapshot, or still, of a previous clip onto a current clip, you can visually assess their differences and similarities in contrast, saturation, and color dominance. In this exercise, you will use stills to manually match clips.

In the green flag-filtered timeline, select clip 05.

In the 02 Balanced Timeline, this clip already has its tonal range and contrast set via the Primaries wheels.

6 Right-click in the viewer, and choose Grab Still.

7 Double-click under the still that appears in the gallery and label it Match Reference.

8 In the timeline, click clip 06. You will be using the Primaries bars and the Parade scope to match this shot to the still.

9   In the Scopes pop-up menu, choose Parade. This representation of the image is similar to the Waveform, but with the luminance value of all three channels represented separately.

10   In the gallery window, double-click the Match Reference still.

You should now see the two clips in the viewer, separated by a wipe line that you can drag.

> TIP You can invert a wipe using the keyboard shortcut Option-W (macOS) or Alt-W (Windows). Doing so will switch the frames for a reverse reference view.

The shot of the man by the fence is of lower contrast and is much cooler than the still with the men and the horse. The Parade scope, which is also split in half, reveals this difference.

The channel traces on the reference still are much more spread out, which is an indication of higher contrast; and the reduced impact of the blue channel in the upper midtones and highlights produces the warmer look of the shot because the complementary color of blue in the additive color space is yellow. The absence of blue in a waveform normally translates to the presence of yellow.

11   In the Node graph, change the label of node 01 in clip 06 to Match.

> TIP Labelling nodes has many benefits. It clarifies the grading workflow by specifying each node's task, which enables you to make faster adjustments as you grade. Labels are also great for inserting reminders to yourself for future returns to the clip grade.
>
> To label nodes faster, consider creating a custom keyboard shortcut to do so. Open DaVinci Resolve > Keyboard Customization and in the lower-right corner of the pop-up interface select All Commands to reveal the full list of Resolve tools. Find the Label Selected Node command in the list below (use the Search field at the top, if necessary), and press the keyboard shortcut you wish to associate with the command. The Tab key is a good option because it is not assigned to any default command.

12   In the Color wheel palette, switch to the Primaries bars.

	Lift				Gamma				Gain				Offset		
0.00	0.00	0.00	0.00	0.00	0.00	0.00	0.00	1.00	1.00	1.00	1.00	25.00	25.00	25.00	
Y	R	G	B	Y	R	G	B	Y	R	G	B	R	G	B

Contrast **1.000** Pivot **0.435** Sat **50.00** Hue **50.00** Lum Mix **100.00**

13   To match the shadows, drag the Lift Y (luminance) bar down until the shadows of clip 06 match the shadows in the still. Keep your eye on the green Parade, in particular, aiming to set the lowest point of clip 05's trace (the man and dog) on a similar level to the shadow in clip 06.

> **TIP** Use the scroll wheel of your mouse to adjust the Primaries bars with more precision.

14   All three Parade traces of clip 06 are higher than the reference still Parades. Drag down the Gain Y bar until the tops of the clip 06 traces are closer to the tops of the reference trace.

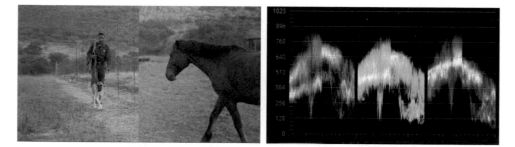

The next step is to address the overall balance to match the reference.

15   Drag down the blue Gain bar until the tops of the blue Parades align.

16   Drag up the red Gain bar to match the warmer reference look.

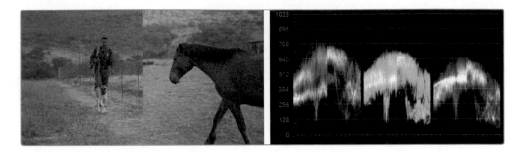

The result is a quick matching of the two clips using the Primaries bars.

17 To turn off the reference wipe view, click the image wipe button in the upper-left of the viewer; or right-click in the viewer, and choose Show Reference Wipe.

18 Toggle the grade bypass to compare clip 06 before and after the manual matching adjustment.

Before match

After match

NOTE The Y (luminance) bar of the Primaries bars affects the image differently than the primaries master wheel. The master wheel affects all RGB channels, which impacts saturation, whereas the bar only targets luminance.

When using stills for shot matching, your grading becomes even more precise when used in conjunction with video scopes. The scopes display a precise measure of the chroma and luma values of each frame, allowing you to make very precise adjustments.

Stills have the additional benefit of carrying the grading data of the clips they were generated from. In later lessons, you will copy this data as a starting point for grading other clips in the timeline.

Comparing and Matching Shots Manually

Unlike the still wipe that you used in the previous exercise, you can grab a reference from any clip in the timeline without generating a still in the gallery. In this exercise, you will extract a reference directly from the timeline and match the images using custom curves.

1   In the green flag-filtered timeline, click clip 04. You will be matching this clip to the previously balanced clip 03.

2   Review the Parade scope for clip 04.

You can see a distinct inconsistency in the shapes of the three channels. The red channel has the widest spread, extending beyond the green and blue channels in both the shadows and highlights. The blue channel's highest point is almost level with the green channel's, even though the blue channel is far more compressed within the midtone range.

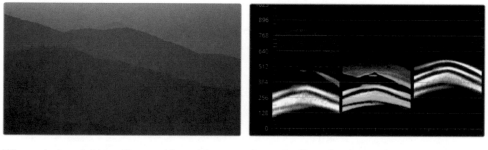

When shot matching, the goal is not to spread out the Parade channels to match each other. Instead, you need to study the relationships of the three channels in the Parade and try to recreate those relationships in the clip that you are matching.

3   Click clip 03, and review the channel relationships within its Parade.

The most obvious difference is in the overall spread and contrast of the channels. The shadows extend to the bottom of the graph, with the red shadows actually touching the black point line (0) and its highlights directly beneath the white point line (1023).

In this situation, visual evaluation of the graph is vital. By understanding the context of the image, you can choose to ignore certain properties of the graph. Clip 09 contains a variety of elements that are not visible in the close-up in clip 10. The trees and field silhouetted against the mountains are portrayed as bunching at the bottom of the parades. You can ignore such elements when using the Parade for shot matching.

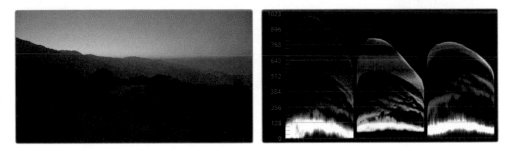

4   Click clip 04.

5   Right-click clip 03, and choose Wipe Timeline Clip.

Both clips become visible in the viewer at the same time, divided by a wipe line.

> **TIP** Quickly toggle the wipe on and off by pressing Cmd-W (macOS) or Ctrl-W (Windows). Some colorists set their reference to fill up the whole screen and toggle the wipe continuously as they match the grade in the active clip.

One way to help you focus on relevant elements of the Parade is to reframe the reference clip within the viewer. Clip 03 is a much wider shot than clip 04, so you can zoom in and reposition it for better reference.

6   Click the sizing button in the middle palettes to open the Sizing palette.

7   In the palette's upper-right corner pop-up menu, choose Reference Sizing.

The reference sizing only applies the transform changes to the reference image in the viewer, not to the actual clip in the timeline.

8   Use the sizing controls to zoom into the reference image by a factor around 6.

9   Pan the image to the left, and tilt down the image as far as you can.

These transform changes place the reference image into a much better position for both visual reference and for the Parade scope.

The side-by-side Parade comparison reveals that the reference image is brighter overall with substantially more influence of the red color in the highlights. The overall spread of the green and blue channels is satisfactory, though they also need to be uniformly raised.

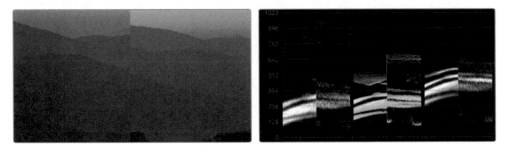

Remember, when matching, it is impossible to recreate the exact shape of the graphs, themselves. Instead, you should focus on matching the height, depths, and the midtone distributions of the graphs.

10   In the Node editor, rename node 01 as **Match**.

11   Open the custom curves palette. Let's perform a few adjustments to see how the curves affect the Parades.

12   Isolate the R curve, and drag the black point up and the white point left until the red channel in both Parades has an equal spread.

13   Isolate the G curve, and drag the white point to the left.

As you drag the green control point, the two other channel Parades shift to compensate, thereby affecting the output of the entire image. This happens because, by default, Resolve tries to keep the luminance of the image constant when you change individual RGB channels in the custom curves and Primaries wheels palettes.

This behavior is usually advantageous when performing creative grades because it maintains the luminance of the image and allows you to adjust only the colors. However, when shot matching, this behavior can be obstructive. To manipulate each channel independently, you need to indicate to Resolve that you do not wish to maintain a constant luminance.

14   Open the Color wheel palette, and choose Primaries wheels as the mode.

15   Select page 1 from the adjustments controls, and drag the Lum Mix down to 0.

> Sat 50.00   Hue 50.00   Lum Mix   0.00

> **TIP** In the Project settings, you can set Lum Mix to default to a value of 0 onevery clip. Go to General Options > Color, and choose Luminance Mixer Defaults to Zero.

16   With the channels behaving independently, you can attempt to match up the curves once again. First, reset the custom curves palette.

> **TIP** When you use the master wheel, you adjust the luminance together with the RGB channels, which impacts the saturation of the image. To adjust only luminance without affecting saturation, press the Option-drag (macOS) or Alt-drag (Windows)the indicator inside the color wheel.

17   Isolate the R curve again, and drag the black and white points until the red channel in both Parades has an equal spread.

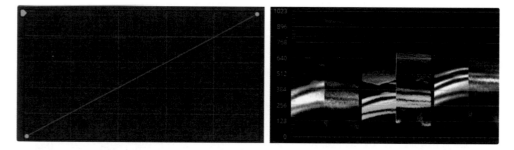

18   Isolate the G curve again, and reposition the black and white points to align the trace in the Parade.

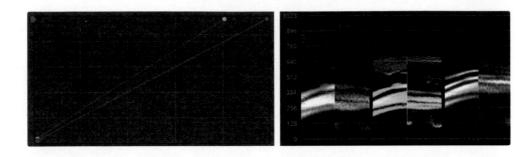

19 Isolate the B curve, and reposition the black and white points to align the trace in the Parade.

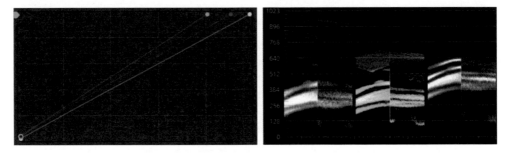

It appears that the Parades now equally match each other, but the colors in clip 04 still do not appear to match the reference. This is because you have been focusing only on the highlights and shadows of the images. The midtones are equally important and can have a profound impact on image appearance.

Notice the bunching occurring in the lower midtones of the channels. It represents the mountains in the image; and though the red and blue channels have been successfully aligned, the green channel is showing a substantial mismatch between clips 04 and 05.

20 Add control points to the green curve, and tweak them until the midtones of the green channel line up more accurately.

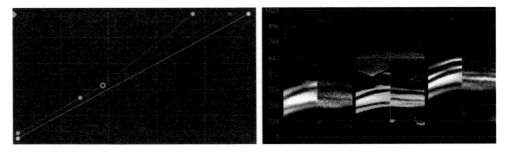

The match between the two Parades results in a satisfactory visual similarity in the mountains and the sky. However, you can now continue to assess the match visually and make further tweaks to refine the result.

The close-up shot could use some contrast to create greater depth between the mountain ranges in clip 04.

21 Tweak the Contrast in the adjustment controls. The depth is now accurate, but the contrast change results in the colors looking more saturated.

22 Slightly reduce the Sat in the adjustment controls.

23 Open the Sizing palette. In the Reference Sizing mode, click the reset arrow to return the reference image to its original placement.

If you do not do this, all future reference images, including wiped stills from the gallery, will have the same transform placement in the viewer.

24 Disable the image wipe.

25 Toggle between clips 03 and 04 to verify that the match is successful.

When matching contrast between clips, you aim to equalize the heights and depths of the pixel spread and match contrast bunching. By displaying an exact readout of the RGB values of each clip, scopes can help you remove the guesswork that might accompany the minute tweaking of midtone ranges and allowed you to approach the image from a more empirical, yet creative mindset.

Using Split-screen Views to Compare Multiple Clips

An alternative method of visually comparing clips within the viewer utilizes a split-screen display. Instead of overlaying the still of a single image, you can display the frames of multiple clips side-by-side. The frames you use could be from other clips in the timeline, stills in the gallery, different versions of grades, or other clips in the same group.

This comparison method is especially effective when you already have a collection of clips that are similar in appearance and wish to examine a wider visual reference of a scene or environment.

1 In the green flag-filtered timeline, click clip 07 in the green flag-filtered timeline. This clip has already been normalized and balanced with custom curves.

2 Shift-click clip 10 to highlight the clips 07 to 10.

3 Right-click in the viewer, and choose Split Screen > Selected Clips to display all four clips in the viewer. For better visibility, press Option-F (macOS) or Alt-F (Windows) to enlarge the viewer.

4   In the viewer, click the upper-right image to select clip 08 on the timeline. The selection is indicated by a white outline in the viewer.

Changes made to the Color page palettes will impact whichever clip is actively selected in the split-screen view. You can perform quick grade matching by switching between clips in split-screen view, visually comparing them and making quick adjustments in the Color wheel and curves.

Although reading the scopes and evaluating their data can be a straightforward process, you must still practice to acquire the level of finesse needed to accurately adjust the colors in the highlights, midtones, and shadows of the image. Accurately adjusting and matching color is a highly valued skillset that requires plenty of practice and patience, so keep at it!

Self-guided Exercises #2

Complete the following exercises in the green flag filtered 02 Balanced Timeline to test your understanding of the tools and workflows covered in this lesson.

Clips 08, 09, and 10 - Match these clips to clip 07 using any of the methods covered in this lesson.

When you've completed these exercises, open the 04 Completed Timeline to compare your matching to the Match node in this "solved" timeline.

Lesson Review

1   How do you prevent changes made to one color channel from affecting the waveform trace of the other two channels?

2   How can you filter the timeline to show only clips with a flag?

3   What does the Pivot in the adjustment controls do?

4   Yes or no? It is possible to use a timeline clip as a reference in the viewer without first creating a still.

5   Which mode allows you to see multiple clips in the viewer at the same time?

Answers

1   Set Lum Mix to 0.

2   Click the Clips button and select Flagged Clips.

3   Adjusts Contrast balance.

4   Yes. To accomplish this, right-click a clip in the timeline, and choose 'Wipe Timeline Clip'.

5   Split screen.

Lesson 3

Correcting and Enhancing Isolated Areas

After you've completed your balancing and shot matching, you will want to target details in the shots for more specific enhancement. This is the secondary color-grading stage.

Secondary color grading is not a standardized phase of the color grading process. Instead, it is a need-driven component of the workflow which is utilized only when a shot requires it. It allows you to achieve a wide variety of goals that help improve the overall aesthetic and creative quality of the footage, as well as to fix continuity errors.

In the first part of this lesson, you'll review some of the more common applications of secondary grading through the use of qualifiers and Power Windows. The goal will be to isolate areas of the Image for color and effect enhancement with the purpose of drawing the viewer's eye.

In the second half, you will use more nuanced tools to clean up overcast (or overblown) skies, to adjust regions of an image based on hue, and to calibrate skin tones to enhance their warmth and even-out detail. Throughout the lesson, you will also employ some of the tools available in the OpenFX panel to see how subtle adjustments can exert enormous effect on the emotional impact of an image.

Time

This lesson takes approximately 90 minutes to complete.

Goals

Controlling the Viewer's Eye

A film's musical score and sound effects can have a resounding impact on an audience perception. Similarly, color and light play a critical role in manipulating the way an audience interprets a scene. In this lesson, you will focus on the fine art of shaping light to control the viewers eye and perceptions.

Drawing Attention Using Windows and Saturation

A simple alteration can dynamically reimagine the composition and mood of a shot by adjusting the saturation of colors. In this exercise, you'll retain the saturation in the vibrant, sunlit area of the field to give the scene a dramatic feel.

1   In the Project 01 - Disunity Documentary project, open the 03 Disunity- Matched timeline.

2   In the Clips pop-up menu, choose All Clips to remove the green filter in the timeline.

3   Filter the timeline to show only clips with yellow flags.

4   In the yellow flag-filtered timeline, click clip 05. The clip already has a first node labelled Normal.

5   Create a second node and label it Sunlight.

6   Click the Window palette located next to the qualifier palette. You will use a window to specify the region of the image you will be grading.

7   Click the linear window button to active it. This is the square-shaped window at the top of the default windows list.

When activated, the button will have an orange outline around it and you will see the outline of the window in the viewer.

8   Double-click next to the window thumbnail, and enter the name **Sunlight Area**.

9   In the viewer, move the four edges of the window to select the entire horizontal middle of the image where the sun hits the ground. Make sure to extend the shape to mimic the path of the sunlight.

10 In the viewer, drag the red points on the window outline to increase the softness around its top and bottom edges.

With the secondary selection created, you can begin to grade the image.

11 In the Color wheel palette, increase the Sat to 65, and the Contrast to 1.1.

> **TIP** Toggle the window outline in the viewer by pressing Shift-~ (tilde) on your keyboard. You can use this keyboard shortcut to hide the outline to better see the impact of your grade on the image.

12 With the Sunlight node still selected in the Node editor, right-click it, and choose Add Node > Add Outside, or press Option-O (macOS) or Alt-O (Windows). This inverse selection will allow you to grade the environment around the sunlight.

13 Label node 03 as Outside.

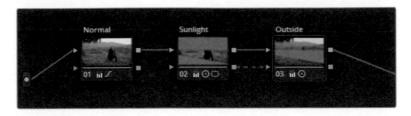

14 Drag the Gamma master wheel (-0.05) to decrease the brightness, and minimize
Contrast (0.900).

Doing so creates a dark framing effect around the figure of the man, and further
draws the eye toward the sunlight on the field.

Before

After

Mimicking a Shallow Depth of Field

ResolveFX are a series of filters included with DaVinci Resolve that enable you to adjust the physical or visual properties of your footage in advanced and creative ways that are often not possible with common grading tools.

> **NOTE** The following exercise requires DaVinci Resolve Studio to complete.

The Tilt-Shift Blur effect imitates the look of a shallow focus lens to direct audience attention. However, you can also apply it to achieve effects that a lens could not, such as reducing focus on elements contained within the same field, and providing a greater level of control over the blur type, amount, and angle. You will continue to work on clip 05 in the yellow flag filtered timeline.

1 Create a new serial node (node 04) labelled Tilt Shift.

2 Click the OpenFX button to open its palette.

3 In the OpenFX panel, locate the Tilt-Shift Blur effect under ResolveFX Stylize.

4 Drag the Tilt-Shift Blur effect onto the empty Tilt Shift node.

The OpenFX library panel will now reveal a Settings window in which you will be able to tweak the Tilt-Shift Blur effect controls.

5 In the settings panel, in the Depth of Field category, select Depth Map Preview to see where the matte is currently located.

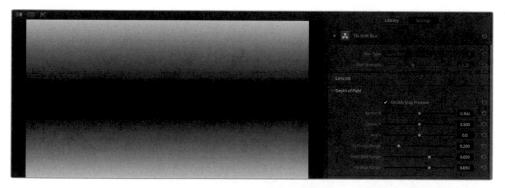

The matte represents where the effect is taking place. Black indicates transparency, or the lack of selection in that area, while white represents full opacity, or a selected region. Grey implied semi-opacity and a diminished strength of selection.

Currently, the map is already placed level with the horizon and successfully targets the rhinos in the background. However, it is not an entirely realistic composite. The depth of field is too extreme at the top and bottom of the image, while maintaining focus on both the man in front of the camera and the rhinos hundreds of yards in front of him.

> **TIP** Repeatedly select and deselect the Depth Map Preview to visually assess the position of the Tilt-Shift Blur matte in relation to the image.

6   Adjust the width of the matte by dragging the In Focus Range pointer to the right (0.330) to include more of the man in the focused range of the shot.

7   Adjust the height of the matte by dragging the Center Y value down (0.460) to ensure that the area directly behind the rhinos begins to go out of focus.

8   Deselect the Depth Map Preview.

9   Slightly decrease the Near Blur Range (0.630) and Far Blur Range (0.630) values to control the severity of the blur and make it look more realistic.

Before

After

Focusing Attention with Vignettes

In classic filmmaking, a vignette refers to the darkened, soft edges of a film frame caused by the lens and matte box. With the advancement of camera equipment, and especially with the advent of digital film, natural vignettes are no longer an issue. However, their absence has caused an appreciation for the framing service they provided, and vignettes are now sought after for creative and compositing purposes as an effective method of directing the viewers eye.

In this simple exercise, you will apply a circle window to a shot and reduce the brightness of the frame around it to create a vignette around the central subject. You will continue to work on clip 05 in the yellow flag-filtered timeline.

1   Create a new serial node labelled **Vignette**.

2   In the Window palette, click the circle window button.

3   Double-click the Layer Name field next to the circle window and enter **Vignette Frame**.

4   Vignettes are usually elliptical in order to reduce their visibility and enable easier blending into the footage, as compared to shapes with straight lines and corners.

Use the onscreen Transform controls to reposition and rescale the circle over the subjects. You will want to create an ellipse that contains both the rhinos in the background and the man in the foreground.

5   In the onscreen controls, drag one of the red points to create a wide, soft edge around the selection.

In the Node editor, the Vignette node thumbnail preview shows that you have selected the subjects. To use the node as a vignette, you will need to invert this selection.

6   In the Window palette, next to the circle window, click the invert symbol.

7   In the pop-up menu in the lower-left of the viewer, choose Off to hide the window outline.

8   Now that the vignette shape has been made, you can proceed to use the grading tools to create a vignette effect on the image. Reduce the brightness of the selected area by dragging the Gamma master wheel to the left (-0.05).

You can also save the vignette you just generated for future use as a preset.

9   In the Window palette, ensure that the appropriate window (Vignette Frame) is selected in the window list.

10 In the upper-right corner of the palette, click the options button, and choose Save as New Preset.

11 Enter the preset name as **Vignette**.

From now on, when you want to apply this exact shape to a node in any other clip, you need only access the Window Palette option menu and choose the preset *Vignette*.

This basic adjustment allowed you to reduce the brightness of the majority of the image to focus attention on the subjects in the center. The softness around the vignette is crucial to ensure that the adjustment does not draw attention to itself.

> TIP Vignettes are most effective when they are not noticeable. If you are concerned that your vignette may be too prominent, review the thumbnail of the clip in the timeline to determine if the vignette can easily be seen in the corners. If so, in the Key palette, lower the vignette node's Key output Gain to reduce its strength and further soften the Power Window edges to more seamlessly blend it into the image.

It takes careful assembly and adjustment of secondary grading to draw the eye of the audience to the subject matter without calling attention to the image manipulation. When an audience becomes aware of the colorist's handiwork, it can break the illusion of realism and compromise viewer involvement with the content.

Using the Mini Panel - Power Windows

Using a DaVinci Resolve Mini Panel enables a great deal of time-saving potential when you're working with Power Windows. To make a Power Window on the Mini Panel, you have a few options. If you'd like to apply a power window to a node, press the Windows button in the upper-left of the panel. The 5-inch screens will display the option of adding whichever kind of Power Window you need.

Then, the knobs allow you to simultaneously adjust the size, pan, tilt, aspect, softness, and opacity of your window. Being able to control pan/tilt, or aspect/softness at the same time allows you to create make more efficient Power Windows more quickly. You can create multiple Power Windows on the Mini Panel, even if they're the same shape. Pressing the Left and Right arrow buttons will cycle between controlling all of the Power Windows you may have placed on one node.

It's important to note that Power Windows extend to the node controls on the Mini Panel. At the upper-right of the panel, node controls allow you to create several types of nodes. You'll learn more about them throughout this book. Right now, you'll want to pay attention to the node + X buttons with which you can create a new serial node with a power window already activated, thereby turning two commonly used shortcuts into one. Pressing the Node + Circle button, for example, creates a new node with a circular power window.

Sharpening Key Elements

The Blur palette in the central palettes of the Color page also contains a sharpening mode tool. It works best when used conservatively and applied at the end of a grade. Too much artificial sharpening can stand out for the wrong reasons. When used precisely, sharpening can make details look extremely dynamic and draw the viewers' eyes in a desired direction.

1   Click clip 04 in the yellow flag-filtered timeline.

2   The clip begins with a man's hand obscuring the shot. In such cases, it is a good idea to play through the clip until you find a better point for grading and adding effects.

In the viewer timeline, drag the playhead to the center of the clip.

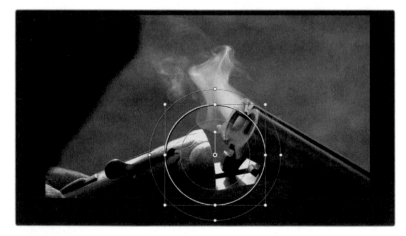

3   Create a third node called Sharp.

4   In the central palettes, open the Blur palette.

5 In the pop-up menu in the upper-right corner of the palette, choose Sharpen.

The main control in the Sharpen palette is the Radius. Dragging it upward will blur the image, and dragging it down will sharpen the edges of high-contrast detail.

6 Reduce the Radius to 0.40 by dragging down any of the three channel sliders under the Radius heading. The three channels are ganged together, so adjusting one will equally alter the other two.

Although it is easy to see the engravings become more detailed, the impact that sharpening has on the rest of the image is more difficult to perceive.

7 Above the viewer, click the Highlight button, and then click the A/B Difference button to display the edges found by the sharpening adjustment. You can also toggle this display on and off by pressing Cmd-Shift-H (macOS) or Ctrl-Shift-H (Windows).

TIP You could also achieve this effect using Sharpen Edge ResolveFX in the OpenFX palette. This filter includes an edge display in the Settings controls, as well as other fine-tuning parameters.

8 In the Sharpen palette, increase the scaling to 0.5. This will multiply the result of the Radius adjustment.

The adjustments add a satisfactory level of detail to the engraving, but too much detail to the gun barrel and the smoke coming out of it. You can limit the sharpening effect somewhat by applying the Coring Softness and Level controls at the bottom of the palette. You can start by increasing the Level control to set a threshold for the sharpening.

9 Increase the Level (around 10-15) until the detail in the smoke and on the barrel of the gun disappears.

10   Increase the Coring Softness to around 5 to recover some of the sharpening between the level threshold setting and the most detailed areas.

To see the results on the image, you can disable the difference highlight.

11   Click the Highlights button above the viewer, or press Cmd-Shift-H (macOS) or Ctrl-Shift-H (Windows).

12   Press Cmd-D (macOS) or Ctrl-D (Windows) to bypass the Sharp node and compare what the original image appearance.

Although the sharpness looks very nice on the engravings, it's causing some ringing on the hand in the left corner of the screen, as well as too much unnatural definition around the smoke. You can use a window to limit the effect to a specific area in the shot.

Tracking Obscured Objects

Adding a simple circular window to the sharpening node will allow you to limit the sharpening on the engravings and rifle barrel.

1   In the Sharp node of clip 04, create a circle window, and name it **Barrel Detail**.

2   Resize the circle, and place it directly over the engravings on the rifle.

3   Make the circle a bit wider and rotate it so it covers both the left-side engravings as well as the right-side open end of the gun barrel.

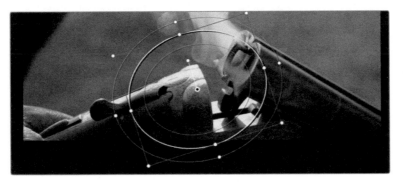

4   Drag the red control point on the window to soften the edges of the mask.

The sharpening has now been successfully isolated to the detail on the rifle. However, scrubbing through the clip will reveal that this is a handheld camera shot, and the rifle is being moved as it is loaded. You'll need to track the window to the rifle for the effect to follow the engravings.

5   In the toolbar, click the tracker button.

6   With the playhead still located in the center of the shot, and your circle window placed on the detail just under the barrel, click the track reverse button.

The analysis runs backward through the shot, recording the motion data for the gun barrel until the first frame of the clip is reached.

> **TIP** It is common practice to track from the center or end of a clip when doing so provides more reliable tracking data.

7   When the tracking is completed, in the upper-right corner of the tracker graph, click the keyframe button to jump the playhead back to the central keyframe.

8   Click the track forward button to perform the rest of the track analysis in the second half of the clip.

As the analysis runs, the window will become disconnected from the barrel detail due to the interference from the man's hand. This can occasionally occur during tracking, and it is useful to know how to quickly fix the issue.

In the Tracker palette, you can see a visual representation of the amount of motion for each transformation. Each colored line corresponds to the colored transformation label above the Tracker palette. Based on the sudden and dramatic movement on the pan and tilt graph lines in the second half of the graph, it is clear that the tracking data becomes distorted. To fix the track, you must first remove the bad tracking data.

9   Drag within the tracker graph to draw a dotted outline around the bad tracking data.

10 In the Tracker palette, in the options menu, choose Clear Selected Track Data.

The tracking data in the selected area of the tracker graph is cleared. Knowing that the track cannot be analyzed with the obstruction, you will need to manually adjust the movement of the window in the time that the hand is in shot.

11 Switch the tracking to Frame mode.

Any changes you make to the window in the viewer will be recorded as a keyframe, as opposed to the Clip mode, which applies a uniform change to the window's position in relation to the clip.

12 In the viewer, drag the playhead to a point in time where the obstruction has passed, and the area appears to be trackable again.

Manually reposition the window to the area of the barrel that you were previously tracking. Use the anchor point in the center of the window as a visual guide, if necessary.

A new keyframe appears in the tracker graph, and tracking data is automatically generated between it and the last reliable tracked moment.

14 Click the track forward button to perform the rest of the track analysis.

Using the Mini Panel – Tracking

The Mini panel can track Power Windows as well. You can avoid using your mouse and keyboard by clicking the tracker button at the upper-left of the panel.

By clicking Frame Mode, you can keyframe Power Windows. Pressing the Left and Right arrows will display more advanced keyframe controls.

Fixing Overcast Skies

Capturing footage with skylines in-camera can sometimes be problematic. Subjects in the foreground usually require a substantial difference in the exposure levels compared to the background sky. Opening the aperture or raising the ISO usually results in better exposure in the foreground, but produces a blown-out sky.

In such cases, the best method of correction is to target the sky with a keying tool, such as the qualifier, and tweak the color using standard grading tools or extract the sky altogether and composite an image/video of another sky in its place. In this exercise, you will practice the first method of sky correction.

1   Click clip 01 in the yellow flag-filtered timeline. This clip was previously balanced and matched, and now needs secondary grading to address its overcast sky.

2   Create a fourth corrector node called Sky.

3   With the Sky node selected, open the qualifier palette in the central palettes.

4   In the viewer, click a portion of the sky with the qualifier tool. The thumbnail representation of the image in the Sky node will change to show the qualifier selection.

To further work with this selection, you must change the viewer mode to display only the qualifier extraction.

5   Switch the viewer to Highlight mode by clicking the Highlight button in the upper-left of the viewer. Ensure that the mode is set to Highlight in the upper-right corner.

TIP   You can toggle the highlight in the viewer by pressing Shift-H on your keyboard.

The viewer now shows what the qualifier has selected by keeping the sky visible and turning everything else gray. This is a way to display the image matte.

Often, when a selection is first made using the qualifier, it will miss sections, or will include unwanted areas. You can use the HSL qualifier palette to fine-tune the selection by dragging the Hue, Saturation, and Luminance sliders to indicate exactly what those respective values should be.

6   Toggle the Highlight button to compare the original image with the selection. You will see that areas of sky between the branches of the trees need refinement.

TIP   It can occasionally be unclear where you should click with the qualifier tool to identify the optimal starting selection. The best strategy is to click close to areas from which you are trying to extract the selection. In this case, the best area is on the horizon directly above the mountains. Once the selection has a clean edge, you can easily isolate the remainder of the area using windows.

Using the Mini Panel – Qualifiers

After you make an initial qualifier selection, you can use the Mini Panel to refine your qualifiers. When you press the qualifier button in the upper-left section of the panel, the two five-inch screens and their surrounding buttons and knobs become the controls you'll use to continue your color grading.

At first, you'll see the controls for Hue on the left screen and Saturation on the right screen. In the upper-left section of the panel, press the Right arrow button to navigate to the Luminance controls. In certain tools, you must use the Left and Right arrow buttons to access all of the functions that a specific tool has to offer.

One more push of the Right arrow button will bring you to the Matte finesse tools.

A good starting point to refining the HSL selection is to disable each value one-by-one to determine if its absence could improve with the qualifier quality.

7   Click the orange toggle next to Hue to disable it.

This has a positive effect on the selection. The horizon becomes refined and more areas of sky in the trees are included in the qualifier result. This result makes sense, because the blown-out white sky is mostly made up of luminance data, not hue.

8   Drag the left side of the Luminance selection (Low) to refine the horizon selection. Aim to include the darker areas of sky between the trees.

The current focus is on ensuring the cleanest possible selection among the horizon; so, for now, you can ignore any other regions in the image that are also selected, such as the horses.

9   In the upper-right of the viewer, click the highlight B/W button to switch to a black-and-white representation of the matte. This is the traditional appearance of mattes, with white indicating full opacity and black representing transparency.

10 You can adjust the Matte finesse controls in the HSL qualifier to further refine the selection. Adjusting Clean Black will reduce some of the minor spill-off occurring in the trees under the horizon. A setting of 20.0 should be enough for a satisfactory reduction.

11 Likewise, tweaking Clean White (20.0) can amplify the white between the tree branches for a cleaner overall selection.

The clarity of the qualifier will often depend on the nature and quality of the footage. In this case, you might experience some minor difficulty in getting a clean extraction from both mountain tops due to the difference in focal length between them. When one mountain has a clean key, the other appears too soft and vice versa. In such cases, the best approach is to break up the keying process into several nodes and combine them using a key mixer.

NOTE You can see the results of using a key mixer to clean up the sky selection on this clip in the 04 Completed Timeline. Open the timeline, right-click the clip, and under Local Versions, choose Mixed Key to see the version of the node pipeline with the key mixer.

Using Windows to Limit Qualifiers

If the HSL qualifier selection has extracted areas of the image that are not the sky, you will want to exclude them from the final matte.

1   Click the Window palette next to the qualifier palette.

2   Click the linear window button to active it. You will see the outline of the window in the viewer.

3   Double-click next to the window icon, and label it Sky Window.

4   Drag its corners around the sky selection to exclude the lower regions of the matte.

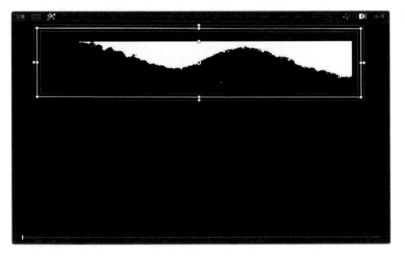

The sky should be now successfully selected and ready for color adjustment.

5   Click the Highlight button to disable the matte preview.

6   Drag the Gain master wheel to the left (0.95) to reduce the overexposure in the sky.

7   Drag the Gain Color Wheel toward cyan/blue to introduce blue into the sky.

TIP You could also use the Color Generator In the OpenFX panel to replace the sky color. It overwrites all the color data in a node with a single color hue without regard for any existing RGB data. It is ideal for working on elements that require a consistent color, but might not be optimal when you are trying to retain some of the natural variations of the hues and shadows in a selection.

Finally, to soften the edges around the tops of the hills, you can gently blur the edge between the black and white portions of the matte.

8   In the qualifier palette, increase the Blur Radius (10.0) in the Matte finesse controls. A gentler edge will ensure a more organic-looking grade and hide any imperfections in the selection.

Adding Atmosphere

When you look into the distance through several miles of air, you start to see the atmosphere reveal itself. In an air-polluted city, the atmosphere may have a hazy white, brown, or orange look; whereas, on a clear day, you would see a soft blue.

When you are enhancing a sky or replacing it altogether, you need to blend a blue hue into the shot's horizon to replicate that atmospheric refraction. Otherwise, the replacement sky might end up looking fake against the horizon.

1   In the Node editor, select and right-click the Sky node, and choose Add Node > Add Outside, or press Option-O (macOS) or Alt-O (Windows). This inverse selection will allow you to blend the color of the sky into the horizon of the image.

2   Label node 05 as **Outside**.

3   With the Outside node selected, in the list of the Window palette, click the gradient window button.

An outline of the gradient controls appears in the viewer in the form of a line with a perpendicular arrow extending from it.

4   In the Window palette, double-click the layer name field next to the gradient icon, and enter **Atmosphere**.

This gradient window works a bit differently compared to the other windows you have created. Instead of defining a shape, you position a starting point and drag the arrow in the direction of the gradient fall-off. The further you drag out the arrow, the softer the gradient will be.

5   Adjust the top of the gradient (the horizontal line) to start at the top of the distant mountain; and then drag the arrow to taper off the gradient toward the bottom.

6   Drag the Offset master wheel in the direction of cyan, but not as far as you did for the sky change. The goal is to give the distant mountain a slight blue tint to convey the blue atmosphere in front of it.

7   Press Cmd-D (macOS) or Ctrl-D (Windows) to compare the results before and after your atmosphere addition.

The gradient looks good in the distance, but covers too much of the foreground mountain. You will want to create a new shape to select everything that you don't want altered by the atmosphere grade.

8   In the Node editor, bypass the Outside node by clicking its number (5). Doing so will allow you to continue work without being distracted by the blue grade.

9   While still in the Window palette, click the Curve button.

10 In the viewer, click around the foreground hill and the lower-half of the frame to create a custom shape around it. To close the loop and define the shape, click the first point you created.

> **TIP** When creating custom windows: click to create linear points, and drag to create rounded Bézier curves.

11 Double-click the layer name field next to the curve button, and enter the name **Foreground**. Enable the Outside node to see the result.

The cyan grade now affects both the background mountain and the entirety of the custom shape. By default, all windows are additive. You will need to indicate that you wish to subtract the selection from the final result.

12 In the curve field, next to the label, click the subtract mask button to extract this custom shape from the final output of the node.

13 To the right of the Window palette, adjust the Softness parameter to feather the edge to the power curve. Drag the Inside and Outside fields to make the border of the window less aggressive between the two mountains.

TIP When changing the sky color, another technique is to use a gradient window on top of the sky selection node. By tapering off the artificial color toward the original hues at the bottom, you can also achieve a realistic-looking secondary grade.

Ordinarily, overblown skies can be addressed on set using ND filters and additional lighting on your talent. However, this solution may not always be an option for smaller productions or documentaries. In such cases, secondary grading becomes a viable option. It keeps the filming process light while ensuring a good shot at the end of the post-production process.

Warping Colors to a Target

On the surface, the Color Compressor filter allows you to select a single hue and flexibly blend it into the image by modifying different color characteristics. The filter begins to offer some impressive versatility when you start combining it with other selection methods, such as the qualifier. The method you'll learn in this exercise can be extremely useful when cleaning up skin tones, hair, and environment to give them a more consistent chromatic appearance.

NOTE This exercise requires DaVinci Resolve Studio to complete.

1   In the yellow flag-filtered timeline, ensure that clip 01 is still selected.

2   Create a new serial node at the end of your pipeline called Grass (node 06).

3   Use the HSL qualifier to select the grass on the ground. Aim to grab a sample of the less vibrant, dry grass. The purpose of the exercise is to adjust the hue to a healthier shade.

4   Tweak the HSL sliders and Matte finesse controls to clean up the selection.

You will notice that the trees are selected almost immediately due to their similarity to the color of the grass. You can temporarily ignore the trees, but pay particular attention to excluding the rhinos from the selection.

5   In the Window palette, create a linear window.

6   Name this window **Grass Matte**.

7   Drag the corners of the window around the grassy field in the foreground of the image.

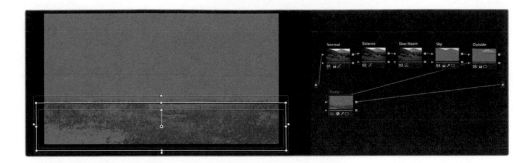

8   Click the OpenFX button to open its palette.

9   In the ResolveFX Color category, drag the Color Compressor effect onto the new node.

> **NOTE** If you are not using DaVinci Resolve Studio, a watermark will appear
> over the image. You can dismiss the warning dialog and continue to follow this
> exercise using the watermarked image.

You can work with ResolveFX more effectively by making the viewer larger and having
the Resolve FX setting panel displayed on the right side.

10   In the Workspace menu, choose Full Screen Viewer, or press Shift-F.

11   In the Color Compressor settings, double-click the box next to the Target Color field,
and select a green hue for the grass.

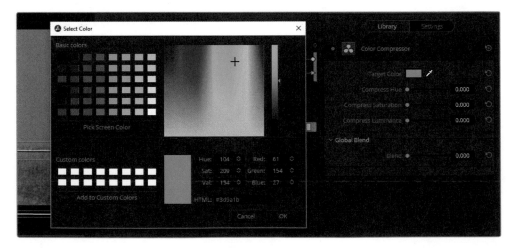

12 Increase the Compression Hue (0.350) and the Compression Saturation (0.050). These changes will increase the amount of the green in the selection and push its saturation.

Before

After

13 When you are done with the adjustments, choose Workspace > Full Screen Viewer, or press Shift-F to exit Full Screen mode.

> **TIP** To remove a ResolveFX from a node, right-click the node, and choose Remove OFX Plugin.

As with all other effects, the Color Compressor can be keyframed, which gives you the ability to enhance a visual detail over time (dull hair grows vibrant, or a dry field turns green). You may also find purely aesthetic applications for the Color Compressor. For example, when compositing, you could blend in a single hue to a backplate clip when a text layer or animation appears over it.

Enhancing Skin Tones with Face Refinement

A very common task for secondary correction is to make skin tones look more natural. Whether you are working with a fictional narrative or a documentary, the audience will be paying the utmost attention to the actions (and, therefore, the faces) of the people on-screen. With this much focus from the audience, you want to be certain that the skin appearance does not cause a distraction.

> **NOTE** This exercise requires DaVinci Resolve Studio to complete.

In this exercise, you'll start with a well-framed and properly exposed shot. The only issue is that the speaker is wearing a wide brimmed hat on a sunny day, which is causing her face to be obscured by shadow. Your goal is to make her face stand out more, and then address general imperfections using the Face Refinement effect.

1   Select clip 02 in the yellow flag-filtered timeline. This clip already has nodes for normalisation (node 01) and balancing (node 02).

2   Create a new serial node by right-clicking node 02, and choosing Add Node > Add Serial, or pressing Option-S (macOS) or Alt-S (Windows). Label the new node Face.

3   In the ResolveFX Refine category, drag the Face Refinement effect onto the Face node.

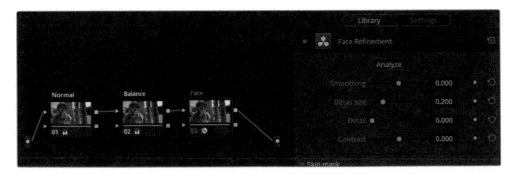

NOTE If you are not using DaVinci Resolve Studio, a watermark will appear over the image. You can dismiss the warning dialog and continue to follow this exercise using the watermarked image.

Face Refinement includes a number of diagnostic and grading tools aimed specifically at enhancing the skin and details of a human face.

The effect analyzes the shot to automatically detect and track a moving face, and to recognize and adjust individual features such as eyes, lips, cheeks, chin, and forehead.

4 In the face refinement settings, click Analyze. Allow some time for processing as the software detects the face and constructs a travelling matte.

When the analysis is complete, you will see a series of green trackers identifying the woman's facial features.

To ensure the highest quality of selection, you should check the matte of the face before proceeding with any adjustments. The matte quality can be compromised when analyzing a subject whose skin tones closely match their hair, clothes, or surroundings. In this example, the subject fits all three of these criteria.

5 Within the face refinement settings, scroll to the Skin mask category, and select Show Mask.

6 Deselect Show Overlay to remove the green trackers.

7 Zoom inside the viewer to get a clearer view of the subject's face.

The selection is very clean overall. The only exception is the upper segment of the mask, which includes part of the tan hat that the woman is wearing.

Combining Windows with Face Refinement

To remove the unnecessary segment from Face Refinement, you will use a window to exclude the top of the matte from the selection.

1   With the Face node still selected, open the Window palette.

2   Create a new circle window, and label it Face.

3   In the upper-right options menu of the Window palette, choose Convert to Bezier to transform the circle's points into Bezier curves. Label the resulting curve window, Face.

4   Adjust the points to fit around her face, paying extra attention to excluding the hat.

5　Deselect Show Mask.

6　Enter the Tracking palette.

7　If you are at the end of the clip, click the Track Reverse button to track the motion of her face backward through the shot.

8　When tracking is completed, refine the mask shape of the mask, if necessary. Return to the Face Refinement settings when you are finished.

Improving Skin Quality

The bulk of the face refinement feature is about fixing skin tones. Skin tones might need adjustment for a variety of reasons:

General skin imperfections, such as variations of color, spots, dryness, oiliness, and so on - By applying the appropriate brightness, contrast, and blurring, you can reduce these issues and put the focus back on the performance.

Some skin types are prone to reflecting light with unpredictable tints - The most common variants are skin types that appear magenta or green under certain lights. The purpose of grading in this case is to remove the tint and match the performer to his surroundings and co-stars.

Overpowering primary grade - When a shot has been extremely graded at the primary stage to look a certain way (for example, to make the environment look cold), the skin can end up looking dead as a result. These kinds of flat grades can drain the shot of life and look dull. By bringing back the skin tone the shot once again becomes vibrant.

In this exercise, you'll look at some of the commonly used settings of the face refinement feature.

1　In the Workspace menu, choose Full Screen Viewer or press Shift-F, to expand the viewer to fill your screen, while still allowing you to access the ResolveFX panel to the left.

2　At the top of the face refinement settings, adjust the Smoothing value to 0.030. Doing so will gently blur the skin to soften minor wrinkles and imperfections.

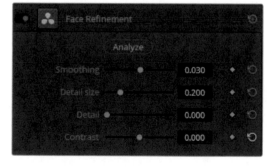

Be careful not to push this setting so far that skin starts to look plastic. You should not aim to remove wrinkles, but merely to soften them.

3   Change the "Detail size" to 0.230 to ensure that larger details on the face are excluded from the smoothing function.

4   Adjust the Detail value to 0.030 to sharpen the smaller details, such as the eyelashes.

5   Finally, set the Contrast to 0.100 to enhance the darker, finer details against the skin.

6   Scroll down to the "Color grading" section to begin work on the woman's skin tone grade.

The Midtone control is responsible for the overall brightness of the skin, which can helpful in negating the presence of shadows.

7   Drag the Midtone slider to the right (0.050) to brighten the skin, but do not pull it so far that the on-screen results become distracting.

"Color boost" enhances the saturation in areas of the skin that are under-saturated.

8   Drag the "Color boost" slider to the right until you reach 0.080.

Tint is responsible for undoing the green or magenta color cast that some skin tones reflect.

9   Drag Tint to -0.200 to reduce the redness in the skin.

10   Next, scroll down to the "Eye retouching" section.

The controls in this section allow you to enhance details in the iris of the speaker, as well as brightening up the reflections from light sources (known as specular reflection).

11   Set Sharpening to 0.030 to refine the pupil, eyelashes, and eye shape.

12   Set Brightening to 0.050 to brighten the color of the iris.

13   Set Eye Light to 0.050 to gently increase the brightness around the eye area.

14   Adjust "Eyebag removal" to 0.200 to brighten the area directly under her eyes.

In addition to addressing general dark circles under eyes, "Eyebag removal" can reduce shadows caused by headwear, as in this clip.

"Lip retouching" allows you to saturate and change the hue of a subject's lip color and to smooth out wrinkles visible in tighter close-ups. As usual, context is key. The park ranger in question is not wearing lipstick, nor do you have a justifiable reason to glamorize her as she talks about the issue of rhino poaching in South Africa. In this case, the "Lip retouching" tool is necessary only to add a minor contrast to her skin tone.

15   Raise the Saturation to 0.200 to define her lips against her skin.

The same guidelines apply to the "Blush retouching" section.

16   Set the Saturation just high enough (0.200) to define her face shape, without making it look like makeup.

17   Additionally, you could expand the Size to 0.500 to spread the gentle redness across either side of her face without concentrating it to the apples of her cheeks.

The final three sections (Forehead, Cheek, and "Chin retouching") enable further hue adjustments to those specific areas. They can be beneficial when employing the traditional portraiture technique of "traffic lights," in which gentle yellow, red, and green hues are applied to the forehead, cheeks, and chin, respectively.

The "Global blend" control at the bottom of the settings allow you to blend the original image back into the Face Refinement node. This is ideal if you are generally happy with your face refinement settings, but find that they are a touch too powerful.

Before   After

With just one node, you have successfully enhanced your subject's skin tone, and made it more pronounced by brightening it, and adding a warm glow. In the original clip, it now becomes apparent how much the shadow of her hat was affecting the visibility of her face and facial expressions.

Adjusting Skin Tones Manually

As impressive as the Face Refinement ResolveFX feature is, it will not work for every skin refinement task. For example, if a face is turned away from the camera, the analysis tool will struggle to locate the facial features. If you are working on a profile shot, you'll need to use the standard selection and grading palettes.

In this example, the subject is under-lit in an overcast environment with shadows on his face that match the depth of the shadows in his clothes and background.

1   Select clip 03 in the yellow flag-filtered timeline.

This clip already has a tonal range and balance set via the Primaries wheels. In Lesson 1, you already used a skin tone to help determine the height of the waveform. Note that the tonal range for the highlights of a darker skin tone rests between 25-50% on the waveform graph.

2   Create a new serial node and label it Skin Hue (node 03).

3   A lens flare is present on the first frame of this clip. To avoid grading on an unreliable frame, drag the playhead to the end of the clip.

One potential approach to adjusting the skin tones of the man is to use the qualifier to extract his skin and treat it as a secondary grade. However, this is not necessarily the best approach. It takes times to create a clean key, and the separation between the skin and the rest of the shot could end up looking too aggressive.

A gentler approach is to use the HSL curves, which will allow you to target his skin range and adjust its hue, luminance, and saturation.

4   Open the custom curve palette, and in the mode pop up menu, choose the Hue Vs Hue curve.

> **TIP** The naming convention of the hue curves describes the selection method, followed by the change type. "Hue Vs Sat" implies that you are targeting a specific range of color to adjust its saturation, whereas "Sat Vs Sat" suggests that you are targeting a certain range of saturation in an image with the aim of increasing or reducing it.

The Hue Vs Hue palette shows all the possible range of hues going left to right. It allows you to sample a specific hue and shift it towards another hue.

One method of hue specification is to use the swatch buttons at the bottom of the curve graph. Another method is to click in the viewer to sample pixel values.

5 In the viewer, click a clear patch of the man's face.

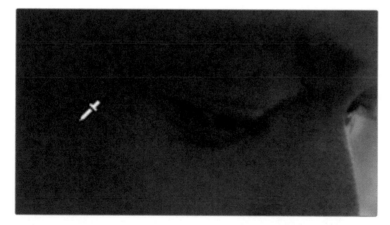

> **TIP** If a hue selection lands near the left or right edge of the palette, the range will smoothly cycle back around to the opposite edge.

Three control points are added to the Hue Vs Hue curve. The center point identifies the selected hue and the control points on either side limit the range of hue that is affected.

6   Drag the center control point down slightly to remove some of the red tint in the man's skin tone. Be careful not to introduce too much green into the skin. If necessary, drag the two control points on either side farther apart to define a wider hue for the skin tone.

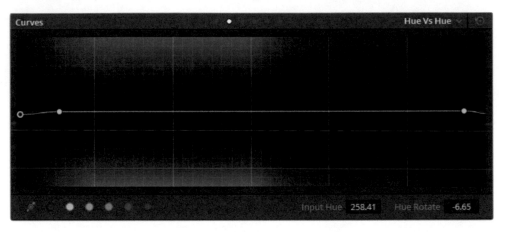

TIP   For more precision when moving a control point, use the Input Hue and Hue Rotation fields in the lower-right corner of the palette.

This may feel a bit like a guessing game. Where is the right hue? To create more certainty in your adjustment, you will need to open the Vectorscope and check what the adjustment is doing to the skin.

The first thing you will need to do is to focus on getting a clean view of the face by removing interfering elements with a window.

7   Open the Window palette.

8   Create a circle power curve window and label it Face Window. Position it over the man's face to isolate a clean patch of skin.

9   Remove the Softness Soft 1 on the window, and click the Highlight button.

This temporary window will aid in providing a clean readout of the skin tone to the Vectorscope.

10 In the Scopes palette, choose Vectorscope as the scope type.

The Vectorscope distributes the visual data of an image on a circular graph representing the hues in the current frame and their saturation levels. A well-balanced image will generally appear as a cloud of pixels in the center of the Vectorscope with some deviations toward specific hues in images that contain prominent colors.

With skin tones, the Vectorscope can be invaluable for determining if a subject's skin is deviating toward the green, yellow, or magenta hues that can look unflattering. The rule is to aim for the skin tone indicator line to ensure normal-toned skin.

11 In the upper-right corner, click the settings icon to adjust the appearance of the scope for easier readability.

12 Drag the Vectorscope luminance slider slightly to the right to increase the brightness of the scope.

13 Select Show 2x Zoom to increase the size of the scope.

14 Select Show Skin tone Indicator to display a line that indicates a healthy skin tone range.

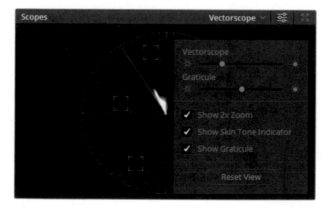

15   Click anywhere on the Color page to close the pop-up window.

16   Drag the center control point in the Hue Vs Hue palette up and down to view the movement in the Vectorscope.

17   Try to move more of the skin data so that it falls closer to the skin tone line.

18   When you are happy with the skin tone hue, turn off Highlight mode to see the entire image, and remove the circle window by clicking the circle icon in the Windows palette.

Perfecting Skin Tone Saturation

The hue of the skin tone is critical because people view skin tones from memory. With an expectation of what a healthy skin tone should look like, the viewer will instinctively know if something is off. You can use another hue curve on a separate node to tackle the saturation of the skin.

1   Create a new serial node and label it Skin Sat (node 04).

2   In the curve mode pop-up menu, choose the Hue Vs Sat.

The Hue Vs Sat palette can be used to make under-saturated items pop and highly saturated items more subdued. When dealing with skin tones, the right settings can be subjective. Generally, darker skin tones require the least amount of saturation (25%), and lighter skin tones require the most (40%) before they begin to look distorted. In this case, the man's skin needs some desaturating.

3 In the viewer, click a saturated patch of the man's face to drop the three points in the Hue Vs Sat curve. Drag the two surrounding control points to include a wider range of the skin.

4 Drag down the central point slightly to reduce the height of the saturation in the Vectorscope.

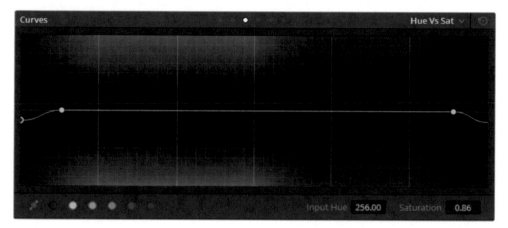

5 Press Cmd-D (macOS) or Ctrl-D (Windows) to disable the Hue Vs Sat node. Press the keyboard shortcut again to view the adjustment.

Memory Colors

Memory colors are colors for which human beings have an instinctive reference. The most common of those are sky, grass, and skin tones, which tend to be closely imprinted in our perception of the world. It is particularly important to grade these colors accurately to ensure audience immersion, unless the narrative specifically calls for a distortion of these hues. Man-made objects tend to have less color memory associated with them, so you have more freedom to tweak the hue of a car or the saturation of a character's dress.

Removing Color Tint in Shadows

Lum Vs Sat is effective when applied to shots with mixed luminance ranges in which color needs to be balanced. For instance, you can adjust a nighttime shot to drop over-saturation in the foreground subjects while maintaining the color of the night sky. Or, a dull daytime sky can be made more dynamic to better match the cityscape below.

In this exercise, you'll remove color tint which ended up in the shadows under your subject's chin.

1   Create a new serial node and label it Skin Shadows (node 05).

2   In the Curves palette, in the pop-up menu, choose Lum Vs Sat.

The Lum Vs Sat palette displays shadows to the left and highlights to the right. You can either click in the viewer, use the swatches, or add a point directly on the graph.

3   Click the black swatch at the lower-left of the palette to place a control point in the shadows range of the image.

4   Drag down the control point to the far left to remove color saturation in the shadows of the image, particularly noticeable under his chin.

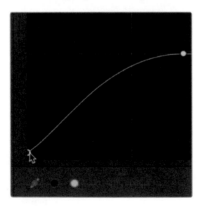

Using the Mini Panel – Hue Curves

When switching between HSL curves, the color presets normally found in the interface are available using the knobs below the Mini Panel screens. You can find additional curves and tools by pressing the Left and Right arrow buttons on the panel.

The hue curves should be your first choices when you are trying to quickly adjust the hue, saturation, or luminance of an object. If the result is not immediately satisfactory, you can then switch to working with the qualifier, which offers a greater degree of control over your matte selection. Also, keep in mind that you can use the hue curves in combination with the qualifiers and Power Windows for an even more refined selection.

Softening Skin

The last step of the skin adjustment exercise is to soften some patchy areas. If you do not have DaVinci Resolve Studio, the midtone detail controls in the adjustment controls of the Color wheel palette is the ideal tool to use. However, the midtone detail can be aggressive on skin texture, and can result in a plastic appearance of the subject.

> **NOTE** This exercise requires DaVinci Resolve Studio to complete.

In Resolve Studio, you have the option of using the Soften & Sharpen effect found in the ResolveFX library.

1   Click the OpenFX button to open its palette.

2   In the ResolveFX Sharpen category, drag the Soften & Sharpen effect onto the last connection line coming out of the 05 *Skin Shadow* node.

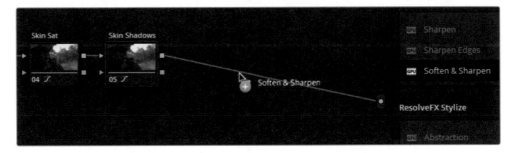

> **TIP** You may need to pan and zoom out on the Node graph by dragging with the middle mouse button to pan, and dragging the slider above the Node graph to zoom out.

Dragging an OFX plug-in or ResolveFX filter onto a connection line will add a OFX/ResolveFX node and connect it into the graph.

> **TIP** You can apply ResolveFX to an existing corrector node or drag onto a connection line to create a ResolveFX node. ResolveFX nodes work slightly differently from normal corrector nodes in that you cannot use grading tools, windows, or qualifiers on a ResolveFX node. They perform only the effect for which the filter was designed.

3   In the Workspace menu, choose Full Screen Viewer, or press Shift-F.

> **NOTE** If you are not using DaVinci Resolve Studio, a watermark will appear over the image. You can dismiss the warning dialog and continue to follow this exercise using the watermarked image.

4   In the Soften & Sharpen settings, increase the Small Texture slightly to reveal more detail in the small creases in the lips and eye lashes.

5   Decrease the Medium textures by a small amount to increase the softness on the majority of the skin.

6   Increase the "Global blend" to mix in more of the original image until the skin appears smoother while retaining a fair amount of detail.

7   Press Cmd-D (macOS) or Ctrl-D (Windows) to disable the Soften & Sharpen node, and press the keyboard shortcut again to view the adjustment.

8   In the Workspace menu, choose Full Screen Viewer, or press Shift-F.

Be careful not to get too aggressive when adjusting skin tones. The aim is not to produce a magazine cover look, but to reduce minor imperfections and enhance the visibility and saturation of the face. Getting too aggressive with the ResolveFX or hue controls can result in plastic-looking skin, which is even more distracting than the imperfections.

Continue utilizing these techniques in new ways and combining qualifiers/Power Windows with your own footage. If you're uncertain how to proceed with a certain shot, write out a workflow to help determine how you want the final output to look, and then work backward to choose the tools and adjustments that will realize your goals. You'll always have several correct workflow options, so experimentation will allow you to learn which are the most visually successful and time efficient for you.

Self-guided Exercises #3

Complete the following exercises in the unfiltered 03 Matched Timeline to test your understanding of the tools and workflows covered in this lesson.

Clip 01 - Use Lum vs Sat in the HSL curves to reduce the saturation of the light under the fence. Increase the overall saturation of the deer shot otherwise.

Clip 04 - Apply a subtle circular vignette at the end of the pipeline in the shot with the rhinos and horses. Create another node before the vignette, and increase the brightness and contrast of the shot to enhance the color and detail.

Clip 11 - Use the Tilt-Shift Blur ResolveFX to create an artificial shallow depth of field in the shot with the man and his dog by the fence. Consider the depth of field in this clip – you might want to rotate the angle of the Depth of Field to be nearly vertical.

Clip 05 - Use the Color Compressor ResolveFX to tint the ground in the field green. Use the greenery in the mountains behind the horses as a reference for the shade of green you should use.

Clip 02 - Apply a window to isolate the rhino's face between the bars, then apply the Contrast Pop effect from ResolveFX to increase the contrast in that portion of the frame. The effect should immediately guide the eye without being overpowering.

Clip 03 - Apply a window and use any of the sharpening methods covered in this lesson (Blur palette, Sharpen Edge FX, or Soften & Sharpen FX) to enhance the numbers on the scale and make them more readable.

When you've completed these exercises, open the 05 Completed Effects Timeline to compare your work to the "solved" timeline.

Lesson Review

1 How are secondary color corrections different from primary color corrections?

2 How is an HSL qualifier selection refined?

3 What does the Hue vs Lum HSL curve do?

4 Which tool can be used to create a vignette?

5 True or False? Track data generated in the tracking palette can be copied and pasted onto another window or node.

Answers

1   Secondary color corrections affect only a part of the image, whereas primary corrections affect the whole frame.

2   Matte finesse.

3   Increases or decreases the brightness of a selected color. The naming convention of HSL curves is that the first word prompts the selection, and the second word affects the change.

4   Circle power window.

5   True. The function to copy and paste track data is found in the options menu of the Tracker palette.

Part 2: Managing Nodes and Grades

Lessons

- Conforming from an XML Timeline

- Mastering the Node Processing Pipeline

- Managing Grades Across Clips and Timelines

In this part of the book, you'll look at workflows beyond primary and secondary color correction stages to improve your speed and productivity when grading. Along the way you'll learn how to conform timelines from other applications, use stills and versions to copy and retain grade data, and perform some common compositing tasks.

Project File Location

You will find all the necessary content for this section in the corresponding folder BMD 15 CC - Project 02. Continue to follow the instructions at the start of every lesson to find the necessary folder, project, and timeline. If you have not downloaded the second set of content files, return to the Getting Started section of this book for more information.

Conforming from an XML Timeline

XML and AAF are two file types frequently used to migrate timelines between different software applications.

However, XML and AAF can occasionally fail to fully migrate timeline structures between different applications dues to variances in software design. Migration inconsistencies can cause problems when you've received content edited in another program and want to grade and finish it in DaVinci Resolve 15. Upon import, you may find that some timeline areas contain incorrect clips, or have failed to migrate transform changes or effects.

To ensure an imported timeline is an exact replica of the editor's work, you must use a verification process known as conforming to compare the reconstructed edit with a reference video to confirm that every cut and effect is reproduced within Resolve. When an element is mismatched or missing, you must manually alter it in the timeline.

In this lesson, you will look at the most common practices and issues associated with the conforming workflow.

Time

This lesson takes approximately **35 minutes to complete.**

Goals

Importing an XML Timeline

The project you will be working on is a film trailer for a documentary called Age of Airplanes. Due to its non-linear nature, you will have more opportunity to experiment with grade construction and more dramatic looks on a clip-by-clip basis.

You will start by reconstructing the project timeline from an XML file exported from the editing software.

1   Open Resolve.

2   Right-click in the Project manager window, and choose Import.

3   On your hard disk, locate the BMD 15 CC - Project 02 folder.

4   In the folder, select the Project 02 – Age of Airplanes Trailer.drp file, and click Import.

> The project is already set up with bins but contains no media or timelines. You will be importing the timelines required for the exercises in this section as XML files and associating the necessary media with them.

5   In the Edit page, select the empty Timelines bin as the destination for the XML timeline, and choose File > Import Timeline > Import AAF, EDL, XML.

6   In the BMD 15 CC - Project 02 folder, navigate to the XMLs subfolder. Locate the Airplanes – 01 LQ Timeline.xml file, and click Open.

> The Load XML pop-up dialog appears in which you can set up how your XML timeline and associated media are treated upon import.

The default settings will work for this project because you want Resolve to find the media that belongs to this XML file.

> **TIP** Selecting "Ignore file extensions when matching" will allow you to choose media that is in a file format different from that of the original timeline media. This option can be extremely useful when switching between offline and online workflows.

7   Click OK to close the dialog.

Resolve will search for the files based on their last known locations in relation to the XML file. Most of the time, drives and paths change during transfer and a dialog will ask for help in locating the missing files.

8   If this dialog window appears, click Yes to locate the missing clips.

9   Navigate to the BMD 15 CC - Project 02 folder, and in the dialog, click OK. This action should reconnect most of your media.

However, one clip will not be found. In this scenario, you've been told that someone renamed one of the video clips after generating the XML file. Due to this change, Resolve has no way of establishing a connection with the media. You will resolve this during the conforming stage.

10 Click No in the second dialog box.

Another window will appear. The Log displays a summary of the migration process, including a confirmation of the imported timeline and a list of encountered issues (translation errors). This summary can be helpful in eliminating some of the guesswork from the conforming process.

11 Read the Log to see the name of the missing clip, and click Close when you are done.

The timeline should now appear in the Edit page, and its media in the Media pool.

12 For easier project management, organize the imported files in the Media pool. The timeline and audio files should be placed into their respective bins, the credits into the Graphics bin, and the video files in the LQ Transcodes bin.

As long as the filenames of media files are not changed, relinking is a straightforward process. For this reason, it is highly advisable to never rename media, but work with the original camera filenames throughout the entire post-production process.

TIP When migratingwith AAF files to and from Avid Media Composer, reel names are another piece of information that you must retain when creating low-resolution dailies and relinking to high-resolution original files. To do so, select the offline clips on the timeline; choose File > Reconform from Media storage; and in the conform options, enable "Assist using reel names from: embedded in source clip file".

Syncing an Offline Reference

With the XML timeline imported and set up, you should now check the edit to ensure that every clip, cut, and effect was successfully migrated. To aid in this stage of the conforming process, the editor should provide a reference movie, a single exported video file of the final timeline that you can use for visual verification of the migrated timeline.

In this exercise, you'll see how you can associate a reference movie with a timeline and fix any issues that may have occurred during migration.

1 Go to the Media page.

2 In the Media pool, select the Reference bin as the target for the new clip you are about to import.

In the Media storage browser, navigate to the BMD 15 CC - Project 02 folder.

4 In the Other folder, right-click the Age of Airplanes REFERENCE.mov file, and choose Add as Offline Reference Clip.

The reference video file is added to the Reference bin in the Media pool, with a checkerboard icon in the lower-left corner designating it as a reference movie.

5 In the Timeline bin of the Media pool, right-click the Airplanes - 01 LQ Timeline thumbnail and choose Timelines > Link Offline Reference Clip > Age of Airplanes REFERENCE.mov.

No obvious change will occur on the screen, but your reference movie is now associated with this timeline. The next step is to display the reference movie in the source viewer for visual comparison.

6 Open the Edit page.

7 In the lower-left corner of the source viewer, in the mode pop-up menu, choose Offline. Doing so will switch the source viewer from showing source materials to displaying offline references associated with the active timeline.

However, the viewer currently shows the red Media Offline frame. One of the most common reasons a reference clip appears offline is because its timecode does not align with the timeline timecode.

If the start timecode is not identical on both the timeline and reference clip, you will often see an offline frame in the viewer.

8 Select the Reference bin, and switch it to list view.

9 In the Start TC column, view the start timecode of the reference clip and compare it against the start timecode of the timeline.

The reference clip begins at timecode hour 00, whereas the timeline is set to start at hour 01. You can easily correct this by changing the start timecode of the reference clip to match the timeline.

10 Right-click the reference clip, and choose Clip attributes.

11 In the Clip attributes window, click the Timecode tab, and enter **01** as the Current Frame hour. Click OK to close the window.

12 If the reference movie does not immediately appear in the source viewer, check the mode pop-up menu in the lower-left corner of the source viewer to ensure that Offline is selected.

With the reference movie and timeline movie displayed side-by-side, you may notice is that the timeline appears more washed out. You can change the color management to remap Log to Rec.709 to give you a more accurate image.

13 Choose File > Project settings, and in the Color management settings, in the "Color science" pop-up menu, choose DaVinci YRGB Color Managed.

14 Set the Input Color space to Blackmagic Design Film, and leave the Timeline and Output Color space fields set to Rec.709 Gamma 2.4. Click Save to close the dialog.

> **NOTE** If the timeline clips do not change when Color Management is enabled, verify that they are not bypassing the Project settings. Select all the clips in the LQ Transcodes bin, right-click, and choose Input Color space > Project - Blackmagic Design Film.

The timeline is now in the correct color gamut, but the reference movie appears over-saturated. Because the reference movie was rendered in a Rec.709 color space, it does not require additional color management and can be bypassed.

15 In the reference bin, right-click the reference movie, and choose Input Color space > Bypass.

Conforming a Timeline

With the reference movie in place, you may proceed with the analysis of the timeline to address any visual inconsistencies. During the first pass you will make sure that the cuts occur at the right time and the clips are in the right locations. To accomplish this, you must review the edit cut by cut.

1 In the Edit page, move the playhead to the start of the Airplanes - 01 LQ Timeline.

2 Press the Down arrow to navigate to the first video cut point, on the start of the second clip on the timeline.

It is apparent that the timeline clip does not match the clip in the reference video. You can import and assign the correct clip to the timeline manually.

3 Enter the Media page.

4 In the Media storage library, navigate to the BMD 15 CC - Project 02 folder, and enter the Other subfolder.

5 From the Other LQ Transcodes folder, drag the AERIAL_SFO_02.mov video clip into the LQ Transcodes bin of the Media pool.

6 Return to the Edit page.

7   In the LQ Transcodes bin of the Media pool, click the AERIAL_SFO_02.mov thumbnail.

8   In the timeline, right-click the second clip, and choose "Conform Lock with Media pool Clip". Doing so replaces the clip in the timeline with the selected source media, which will now match the one in the reference movie.

> **NOTE** If the clip in the Media pool and the clip in the timeline have the same timecode, the conform action will place the incoming clip using the same in and out points as the original cut. If the timecode doesn't match, the first frame of the incoming clip will be aligned at the cut.

Fixing Translation Errors

You can continue to navigate down the timeline and look at the reference movie to check the clips, edit points, and effects to ensure everything has been successfully translated.

1   Press the Down arrow to jump to the next video cut at the start of clip 03 TAKE_OFF_SFO.

Together with checking the clips on the timeline and their edit points, another aspect of conforming is ensuring that all transitions and effects have carried across. This cannot always be easily verified in a side-by-side comparison, so you have the option of superimposing the reference movie on the Timeline viewer. This helps to verify if the clips are framed identically.

2   Right-click the timeline viewer, and choose Horizontal Wipe.

The timeline clip is displayed to the left while the reference clip is displayed to the right.

3   Drag the wipe left and right to compare the placement of the clip to the reference.

Using the wipe for comparison reveals a mismatch in the framing of the shot. To fix it, it would be easier to show a difference composite.

4   Right-click the Timeline viewer again, and choose Difference to highlight where the clip is misaligned.

5   In the timeline, click the 03 TAKE_OFF_SFO clip, and open the Inspector.

6   In Transform controls, increase the Zoom value until the size of the cockpit windows appear the same (1.200).

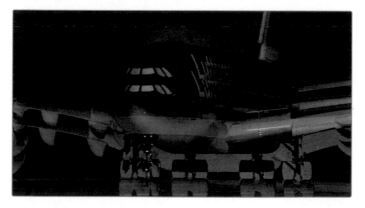

7   Because the windows and wings appear higher in the timeline, drag the Y position down (-100.00) until the windows and wings overlap. When performing these matches by eye, you will need to go back and forth between the position parameters to get a perfect fit.

The difference image should become appear black to signify that no visual differences remain between the clips.

8   Right-click the timeline viewer, and choose No Wipe to return to the normal timeline viewer. Close the Inspector to bring back the offline reference viewer.

9   Press the Down arrow to navigate to the next video cut. This is the missing clip that was not found when the XML timeline was being imported.

10   Switch to the Media page, and in the Media storage browser, locate the Other folder, and open the Other LQ Transcodes subfolder.

11   Drag the BA4662_54 and BA4662_55 clips into the LQ Transcodes bin of the Media Pool, and return to the Edit page.

In the timeline, one of the imported video clips will replace the missing media. However, the clip does not match the reference movie in the source viewer. In the lower-left corner of the timeline clip, an attention badge icon indicates a potential metadata clash with another clip in the Media pool.

NOTE If you do not see the red attention badge icon next to the clip name, it might be because the clip is conform locked on the timeline. If so, right-click the clip, and choose Conform Lock Enabled to disable the lock. You can now access all clips that are associated with its metadata.

12   Double-click the attention badge on the clip.

The conflict resolution window appears, displaying all the clips in the bin that match the metadata of the clip in the timeline. You can now select the correct clip according to the reference movie.

13 In the conflict resolution window, select the water shot BA4662_55 to change the media, and click Change to apply.

The correct clip is placed in the timeline to match the reference movie. To remove the now black resolved badge and confirm the new clip as the correct one, you can lock the conformed selection.

14 In the timeline, right-click the clip, and choose Conform Lock Enabled.

15 Continue to press the Down arrow to check the remainder of the clips.

When you reach clip 08 (YELLOW_PLANE), you will notice that the clip has very different colors compared to the reference movie.

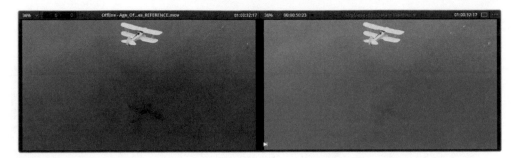

It is common practice for editors, DPs, or other creative directors to leave preliminary grades baked into the reference movie as a guide for the colorist. As a general rule, grading data does not come across in migration files unless the project is sent as a DRP file, or it includes accompanying LUTs or CDL data.

It will not be necessary to do anything with this clip at this time, but it will become useful when you begin the grading process.

Though it is natural to feel that something has gone wrong with your workflow when the timeline presents issues during XML migration, it is important to remember that this is a completely normal and anticipated stage of post-production. It is encountered in projects of all calibers and stems from the fact that no single migration standard exists among the dozens of programs that may be used when collaborating on a film project.

One of the major advantages of performing your entire post-production workflow in DaVinci Resolve 15 is a substantial reduction of migration and project management issues. An edit can be ingested, edited, graded and delivered without ever needing to be conformed.

Associating HQ Footage with a Timeline for Online Workflows

The timeline you reconstructed for this section is currently associated with media from the LQ Transcodes folder. These are low-quality video files generated from the source media with the intention of providing the editor with light video files that are easy to transfer and do not lag when played back in real-time.

The accuracy of an image's pixel data is not as vital to editors because they are focused on constructing a narrative and getting a good flow in the edit. However, when the timeline reaches the colorist, the quality of the image becomes paramount. You will want to create a copy of the timeline that links to the HQ video files, optimal for grading.

1   In the Edit page, in the Media pool, open the Timelines bin.

2   Right-click Airplanes – 01 LQ Timeline, and choose Timelines > Duplicate Timeline.

3   Double-click the name of the new timeline, and rename it **Airplanes – 01 HQ Timeline**.

4   Double-click the HQ timeline to open it in the Edit page timeline window.

5   In the Media pool, click the empty HQ Transcodes bin to select the destination for the HQ media.

6   Drag to select all the video clips in track V1 on the timeline. Do not include the credits in your selection.

7   Right-click any clip in the timeline, and deselect Conform Lock Enabled to disable the clips' lock on their media file paths and prompt them to acknowledge all media that shares similar metadata and timecodes in the Media pool.

8   In the File menu, choose Reconform from Media storage.

The Conform from Media storage window allows you to refine the nature of the media that is being associated with the clips in the timeline.

9   Under Chose Conform Folders, select the BMD 15 CC - Project 02 > HQ Transcodes folder.

10 Under Conform Options, deselect Timecode.

11 Select File Name, and keep Tight filename match as the option.

12 Click OK.

The HQ Transcodes bin is populated with the higher-quality clips that have also replaced the LQ clips on the timeline.

13 To check that the link was successful, in the HQ Transcodes bin, select all the newly imported clips. Right-click one of them, and choose Clip Color > Orange. All the clips in the timeline that were successfully switched to the higher-quality media will appear orange in the timeline.

Before

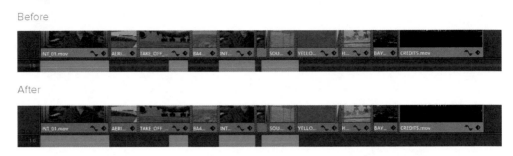

After

14 If the clips in the viewer have reverted to the Log color space, in the HQ Transcodes bin, select all the media. Right-click, and choose Input Color space > Project - Blackmagic Design Film.

15 To lock the HQ clips to the timeline, select them, right-click, and choose Conform Lock Enabled.

This method of changing file source locations gives you full control over the media used in the timeline without the need to import additional XML files, or to change the file paths of the clips in the Media pool. An important component of this workflow is a well-organized and consistently labelled file system, which is vital in all post-production workflows.

Having successfully imported and prepared the XML timeline for grading, you can proceed with the knowledge that the timeline is accurate, and you are in control of the quality of your footage at all times.

Lesson Review

1 During project migration, what is a 'translation error'?

2 How do you appoint a video file as an offline reference movie?

3 Yes or no? Will Resolve Color Management affect an offline reference clip?

4 When loading an XML file, why would you sometimes opt to 'Ignore file extensions when matching'?

5 What does File > Reconform from Bins allow you to do?

Answers

1   When there are inconsistencies in a reconstructed timeline between programs.

2   In Media Storage, right-click the video file and Add as Offline Reference Clip. Then right-click the timeline and select Timelines > Link Offline Reference Clip.

3   Yes, it will be treated like any other visual media in the project.

4   This will allow you to specify which media (offline or online) to use in the timeline reconstruction.

5   Change the source of the media based on a different bin in the Media Pool.

Mastering the Node Pipeline

The Node editor is a powerful component of the Color page that allows you to maintain precise control over the final appearance of your images. With it, you may separate and target different stages of grading, ensuring an enhanced color output with minimum quality degradation. Additionally, it enables some truly complex secondary grading configurations, the foundations of which you will explore in this lesson.

Time

This lesson takes approximately 60 minutes to complete.

Goals

Understanding Node-based Compositing

Node-based compositing is different from the layer-based system familiar to many NLE editors. Unlike layers, in which the visuals are compounded based on their order in the layer stack, nodes process a single RGB signal, modifying it along the way.

As each node affects the image, it outputs the altered signal via an RGB link until the final RGB data reaches the output node of the Node editor. This output node represents the image in its final state and is what the colorist sees in the viewer, and how the media will look upon being rendered.

Nodes are capable of reusing information from previous nodes, substantially reducing the amount of processing power required to assemble and output a final image. This is particularly useful when working with keys, such as those generated by qualifiers and Power Windows.

The Anatomy of a Node

The Node graph is read from left to right. The RGB signal that constitutes the visual information of the image beings at the leftmost green node, the RGB input, and travels via the links that connect the corrector nodes until it reaches the final node tree output on the right-hand side. The RGB signal must be uninterrupted for the grades to be correctly compiled and output.

Standard corrector nodes have two inputs and two outputs.

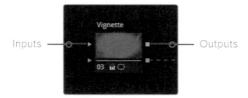

The green triangle and square shapes at the top of either side are the RGB inputs and outputs. These carry the pixel data of the image, which is manipulated within the node using the grading tools of the Color page. Corrector nodes can only accept one RGB input but can output multiple RGB signals to other nodes.

The blue shapes are the key inputs and outputs. These enable you to transfer the key data generated by the Power Windows and qualifiers (or external mattes) to be used by other nodes.

> **NOTE** You can undo an action in DaVinci Resolve 15 using the shortcut Cmd-Z (macOS) or Ctrl-Z (Windows). The undo function is stacked to each clip in the timeline. So, when you undo, only the changes from the selected clip are removed, and not from any other clips on the timeline, even if you graded them more recently.

Understanding the Importance of Node Order

The RGB signal output of each node carries the full weight of its grade and directly affects the next node's interaction with it. The following set of exercises are designed to demonstrate how nodes impact one another.

> **Node Order Demos**
>
> The node structures of every exercise in this segment can be found in the "Node demos" album of the gallery in the Color page.

Influence of Color and Saturation Across Nodes

A straightforward demonstration of how a node at an early pipeline stage influences the nodes that follow it is to remove its saturation and observe the effect.

1 Open Project 02 – Age of Airplanes Trailer project.

2 Enter the Color page.

3 Click clip 01 in the Airplanes – 01 HQ Timeline.

4 Label the first node *BW*.

5 Open the RGB Mixer palette, which is located next to the Color wheel palette.

6   Select Monochrome at the bottom of the palette to turn the image black and white.

The RGB Mixer gives you full control over the strength of the individual RGB channels and is often used for tweaking black-and-white images to create an aesthetically pleasing balance of natural elements such as skin, sky, and trees.

7   Drag up the red output's R bar to increase the strength of the red channel in the image. This change will brighten the man's face against the background, and create a good contrast.

8   Create a second node and label it Sepia.

9   Open the Color wheel palette and drag the offset color wheel towards orange-yellow to give the image a sepia look.

10   Click node 01 BW, and return to the RGB Mixer palette.

11   Drag the blue output's B bar up and down to increase and decrease the strength of the blue channel in the image.

The effect this has on the final sepia grade demonstrates that the luminance and contrast created in the first node continue to impact the image even after a second node has dramatically changed its appearance.

For an even clearer visualization of how the node order impacts the grade, you can switch the order of the two nodes around.

12   Click node 02 Sepia, and press E to extract it from the pipeline.

13   Drag the disconnected node onto the link in front of node 01 until a + (plus sign) appears.

TIP   A quick way to switch the order of two nodes is to Cmd-drag (macOS) or Ctrl-drag (Windows) one node over another.

When reconnected, the image becomes black and white. Though the Sepia grade is still performing its function in the first node, it is being completely overwritten by the BW node, which is turning the RGB signal monochromatic and sending it to the node tree output.

Adjusting Contrast and Luminance on Nodes

Understanding the function of the RGB inputs and outputs more clearly, you can now check how mild adjustments to luminance and contrast can still have substantial impact on an image.

1   Press Cmd-Home (macOs) or Ctrl-Home (Windows) to reset the grade in clip 01.

2   Label the first node Lift.

3   In the Color wheel palette, drag the Lift master wheel to the left until it reaches -0.25.

4   Create a new node, and label it **Curves**.

5   Open the curves palette and ensure that the YRGB channels are linked.

6   Click the center of the curve to create a new control point, and drag it up to brighten the image.

The clip becomes severely distorted. The fine detail that was contained in the shirt is crushed by the contrast, and the face becomes patchy and over-exposed. This is an example of a "destructive" workflow in which the changes made in one node have clipped and restricted the RGB data used by the following nodes.

Thankfully, you cannot really destroy RGB data in the pipeline. By using the correct part of the curve, for example, you can fully restore the data of the original image.

7   Right-click the center control point on the curve to remove it.

8   Drag the black point of the Y curve upward along the left side of the curves graph. Stop when you are just under the second horizontal line from the bottom.

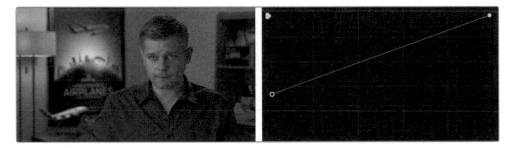

The black point of the curve is equivalent to the Lift master wheel, which is why you were able to retrieve the details that it crushed. By dragging the center of the curve, you were impacting the gamma range, which targets a very different range of luminance.

Though you were able to restore the image in this instance and continue using the previously crushed shadows, you can probably imagine how more subtle changes to the brightness and contrast of an image in early nodes could impact the quality of adjustments made to the shadows and highlights in later nodes.

It is important to keep in mind the potential of engaging in destructive grades. As a general rule, balancing, matching, and secondary grades should come before bold contrast adjustments and sweeping creative grades. It is far more acceptable to distort and crush data in final nodes because no other nodes rely on them for RGB info.

Another consideration when grading is choosing the order in which to apply color changes to an image. In this scenario, you are trying to create a clip with a distinct blue cast, while retaining control over the skin tone in a subject's face.

1   Reset the grade on clip 01.

2   To save time, the balance node for this clip was already created. Open the gallery, and ensure that the Stills Albums button is enabled to show a list view of the available albums.

3   Open the "Base grades" album, and apply the INT 1 Balance grade to the clip.

4   Create a new node called Blue look (node 02).

5   In the Color wheel palette, drag the Gain and Gamma wheels toward the blue-cyan range to cool down the image, and then counteract the blue dominance in the shadows by dragging the Lift wheel slightly toward red.

6   Use the Contrast and Pivot settings to refine the contrast and brighten the upper midtones of the image. Aim to create fine shadows on the man's shirt.

7   Finally, reduce the Saturation to 40 to remove the blue vibrancy and end up with a cold, desaturated image.

This look has a strong, purposeful design. It could effectively convey a somber mood or suggest a different point in time in a non-linear narrative. However, its impact on the speaker's skin tone reduces its effectiveness and could end up being tiring to the eye.

8   Create a final node called Skin tone (node 03).

The man's face is close in hue to the color of the wall behind him, so using HSL curves might not be the most effective choice. A qualifier selection would give you a better chance of isolating the skin in this shot.

9   Open the qualifier palette, and click the man's face to grab a sample.

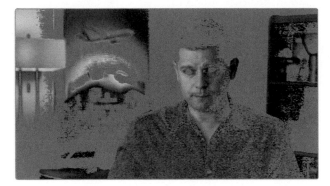

Due to the RGB signal passing through the Blue look node, the qualifier is forced to work with a very cold, contrasted version of the man's skin. This is definitely not an ideal point in the timeline to be keying skin, or to be grading it.

10   Select the Skin tone node, and press E to extract it from the pipeline.

11   Drag it onto the link between nodes 01 (Balance) and 02 (Blue look).

12   Reset the qualifier on the Skin tone node and select the skin again. In the qualifier window, adjust the HSL and Matte finesse controls to get the best extraction. Remember to turn on the Highlight mode in the viewer to best observe the end result of the selection.

This time the qualifier gives you a much better result.

NOTE   The qualifier continues to be actively influenced by the nodes preceding it. Changing the hue or brightness of an earlier node at any point of the grading workflow will impact the selection (and quality) of the qualifier.

13 Use the Window palette to isolate and refine the selection of the man's face.

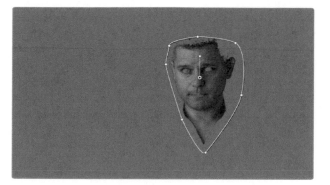

14 In the viewer, turn off the Highlight mode.

15 In the adjustment controls, raise the Sat of node 03 Skin tone to 55, and drag the Offset wheel slightly toward orange.

Overall, the resulting grade is much more acceptable. You were able to derive a clean qualifier key for the skin tone and adjust it to act as a visual contrast to the blue grade. However, because Blue look is the final node to impact the image before the node tree output, you know that the original skin tone hues will always be tinted blue no matter how much you grade the Skin tone node.

This exercise demonstrates how you could actively decide on the placement of nodes based on your RGB needs. For example, when using a qualifier, you almost always want to work with the ungraded or balanced version of the image, free from any severe color or contrast impact.

In the upcoming exercises, you will see examples of how you can derive primary and secondary grades from the same point in the node pipeline and recombine them with the help of mixer nodes.

Creating Separate Processing Pipelines with a Parallel Mixer Node

Mixer nodes allow you to combine multiple nodes into a single RGB output. The two mixer node types, parallel and layer, have identical structures but process the incoming node data differently.

The Parallel Mixer combines grades by blending them to an equal degree. The result appears similar to working on a linear node pipeline, with the main difference that nodes are able to extract RGB data from the same point in the node tree.

1   In Airplanes – 01 HQ Timeline, click clip 01.

    You will continue to work with the grade you constructed in the previous exercise. This time, the Blue look and Skin tone nodes will be placed alongside one another for the most optimal routing of the RGB signal between them.

2   Right-click node 02 Blue look, and choose Add Node > Add Parallel, or press Option-P (macOS) or Alt-P (Windows), to add a Parallel Mixer node.

    A new corrector node (node 05) is created, as well as a Parallel Mixer node that combines the RGB outputs of the two nodes before it.

3   To reuse the qualifier selection of the skin tone, you can select node 02 Skin tone and press Cmd-C (macOS) or Ctrl-C (Windows) to copy the node data.

4   Select node 05 and press Cmd-V (macOS) or Ctrl-V (Windows) to paste.

5   With the qualifier copied, you can delete the old node 02 Skin tone. For organizational purposes, you can rename the new node located under the Blue look node to Skin tone.

    You now have a node structure in which both the Blue look and the Skin tone nodes are using the same RGB data from the Balance node. Their respective grades are then combined at equal strength in the Parallel Mixer node. The mixer sends out a single RGB link to the node tree output.

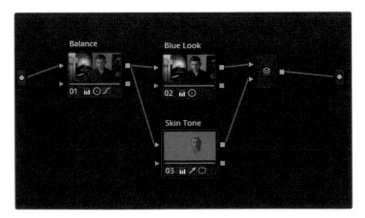

In the viewer, you should notice a subtle change to the skin tone. You no longer have a blue hue on the highlights of the man's face, and the overall color appears warmer. If the appearance is too dramatic, you can select the Skin tone node and reduce the Sat value in the Color wheel palette or pull the Offset Color Wheel point closer to the center.

Skin tone adjustment using:

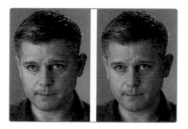

Linear nodes   Mixer nodes

The Parallel Mixer is perfect for performing organic, or natural-looking adjustments such as skin tone or hair work.

Morphing Mixer Nodes

An alternative to Parallel Mixer nodes is the Layer mixer node. The next few exercises will demonstrate the differences between the two in more detail; but in the meantime, you will morph the current clip's Parallel Mixer into a Layer mixer node to see the impact this will have on the image.

1   Click clip 01 on the Airplanes – 01 HQ Timeline.

2   In the Node editor, right-click the Parallel Mixer node, and choose Morph into Layer mixer Node.

This change has a jarring effect on the image. The skin tone now appears far less realistic and the edge around the face is harsh and solid. This is because node I03 Skin tone is now being treated as an RGB image layer. The keyed face has 100% opacity and is overlaid onto the node 02 Blue look image underneath.

In its current state, the grade is unusable. However, by making an adjustment to the opacity of the skin tone layer, you can still blend it into the Blue look layer.

3   Select node 03 Skin tone.

4   In the central palettes, open the Key Mixer palette.

5   Enter the Key output Gain as 0.5 to reduce the opacity of the skin tone node by half.

The face now blends much more naturally into the blue background node.

Both parallel and Layer mixer nodes provide an easy option to morph them from one state to the other. This makes it easy to experiment with grade structure and find the optimal balance and blends of nodes.

Having seen a demonstration of how to switch between the two nodes and how differently they affect an image, let's look more closely at how the mixers operate to gain an understanding why and when you would choose one mixer over another.

Visualizing Mixer Nodes

A simple way to familiarize oneself with how Layer mixers operate is to create a basic RGB graphic setup that will clearly demonstrate the relationship between the nodes.

1   Enter the Edit page.

2   Open the Effects Library by clicking the button at the top of the page.

3   Inside Toolbox > Generators, locate the Grey Scale generator.

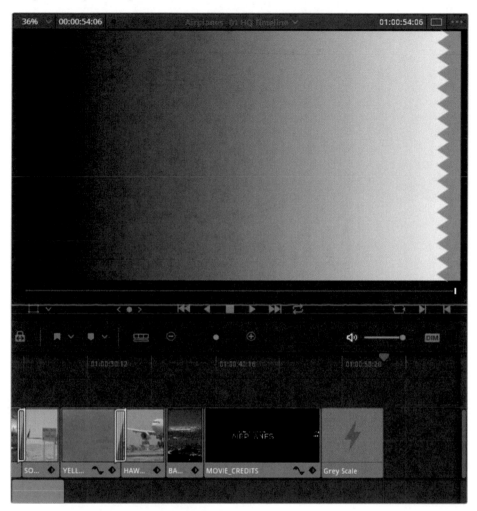

To work on the generator in the Color page, you first need to transform it into a compound clip, so it can take on video properties.

5   In the timeline, right-click the generator, and choose New Compound Clip.

6   Name the compound clip **Grey Scale**.

7   Enter the Color page.

8   With the generator clip (clip 12) selected, create a new serial node.

9   Right-click node 02, and choose Add Node > Add Layer, or press Option-L (macOS) or Alt-L (Windows), to add a Layer Mixer node.

10   With node 02 selected, create another layer node to produce a stack of three layer nodes.

11   Label the nodes (from top to bottom) Red, Green, and Blue.

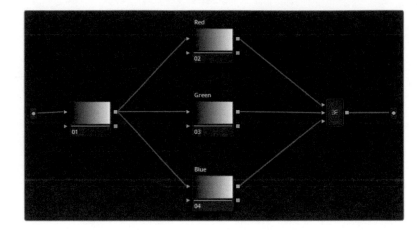

12 Select the Blue node.

13 In the central palettes, open the Window palette, and click the circle window button to create a circular window.

14 Open the RGB Mixer palette, and make the circle blue by dragging up the B bar of the blue channel.

15 Move the circle window to the lower-right of the viewer. Your goal is to create three intersecting circles (red, green, and blue).

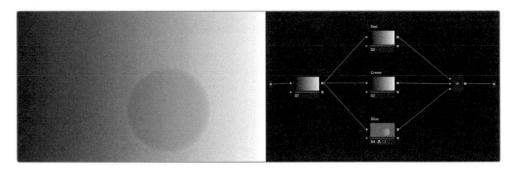

16 Select the Green node and also create a circle window in it.

17 In the RGB Mixer palette, make the circle green by dragging up the G bar of the green channel.

18 Move the Green node window to the lower-left of the viewer.

19 Finally, create a red circle in the Red node. Turn it red using the RGB Mixer and move it to the top.

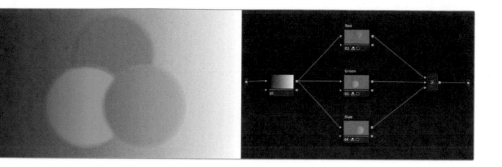

This end result demonstrates how nodes interact when combined in a Layer mixer node. Their behaviors are reminiscent of layer-based systems in which the upper RGB input of the Layer mixer constitutes the lower layer and is compounded by each subsequent RGB input. The default status of the nodes is full opacity.

20 Right-click the Layer mixer node, and hover over the options in the Composite submenu.

Doing so will allow you to preview how the colors of the nodes will interact under the different hue and luminance blending methods. Note that all the top nodes are blended until they reach the bottom layer (Red), which remains at full opacity.

21 Select Lighten to apply the Composite mode.

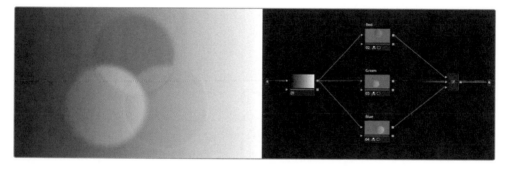

22 To remove the Blend mode, right-click the Layer mixer node, return to the Composite menu, and choose Normal.

Next, you'll change the order of the node layers.

23 Move your mouse over the link between the Red node and the Layer mixer to reveal the blue highlight. Drag the link to the bottom input of the Layer mixer to disconnect the Blue node from the Layer mixer.

24 Drag the RGB output of the Blue node toward the top input of the Layer mixer.

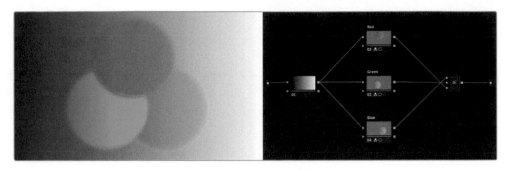

The red circle now overlaps the green and blue. This further demonstrates how the RGB input order in the mixer node works. Additionally, it emphasizes that the physical location of the nodes in the Node editor has no impact on the grade and the final result in the viewer.

25 To compare the interaction of the circles in the Parallel Mixer, right-click the Layer mixer node, and choose Morph into Parallel Node.

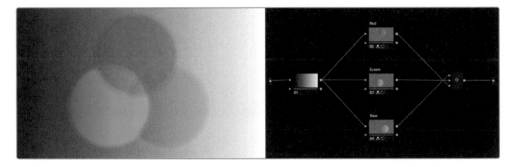

This operation changes the behavior of the three circles. Instead of treating the layers at full opacity, it adjusts their transparencies to show an equal amount of each. Unlike a blend mode, their luminance values are not targeted.

The composite blending options in Layer mixer nodes can produce very dynamic looks. You can use them to emphasize some areas of your shots, or even to compile graphic design elements.

The Parallel Mixer is ideal for applying realistic-looking grades on nodes that are seamlessly blended into one another while deriving their RGB data from the same level in the node pipeline.

Compositing Effects with the Layer Mixer Node

In this exercise, you will use a Layer mixer to construct an image that has several secondary grading needs. Unlike the interview example, the focus will not be on seamlessly blending the colors of the image into each other, but to work on each distinct element separately.

1   Click clip 8 in Airplanes – 01 HQ Timeline.

In the previous lesson, the reference timeline indicated that the water in this clip needed to be turned blue.

You have several ways to approach this secondary grade. You could use HSL curves or the qualifier, together with the RGB Mixer, wheels, or custom curves. When confronted with a specific grade problem, it is common to cycle through several options until you find the optimum grading solution. In this instance, you will use a combination of techniques, including the 3D qualifier and custom curves.

2   In the viewer, drag the playhead closer to the end of the clip to better see the plane against the water.

3   The end of clip 08 is in mid-dissolve with the following clip 09. To disable transitions and effects that are on the timeline in the Edit page, click the Unmix button in the lower-left of the viewer.

4   From the "Base grades" album in the Gallery panel, apply the 1.8.1 Balance still to normalize the luminance of the clip on the first node.

5   Create a second node and label it Blue Water. You will use this node to turn the image blue, with focus on getting the correct blue hue in the water.

6   In the custom curves palette, isolate the B channel, and drag its black point up the vertical plane until the water is a rich blue color.

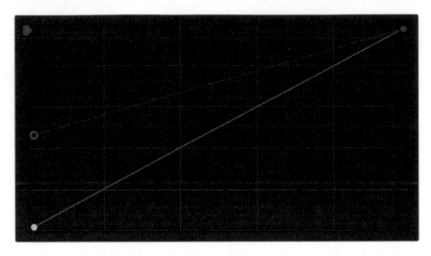

7   To check how the graded image compares to the reference, right-click in the viewer, and choose Reference Mode > Offline. Then click the Image Wipe button in the upper-right corner of the viewer.

8   Lower the Gamma master wheel to control the brightness of the water.

9   Drag the Sat and Hue adjustment controls to get the right water temperature.

Note that the plane will also be affected by these grade changes. That is acceptable because in subsequent layer nodes you will extract the plane and grade it separately.

10   Press Option-L (macOS) or Alt-L (Windows) to add a Layer mixer and a new node (node 04). Label the new node *Yellow Plane*.

11   Open the qualifier palette, and change the mode from HSL to 3D. This is the recommended qualifier mode for chromakey work due to its ability to intuitively predict hue and shadow fluctuations on green screens.

12   In the viewer, drag the qualifier across the green water to make a selection. You can repeat this action as many times as necessary to build a reliable chromakey reference.

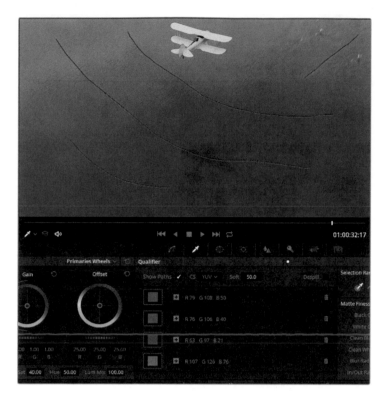

Every time you create a color sample, a swatch is placed in the 3D qualifier list to document the hues that are included in the selection.

13 When finished, enable Highlight mode in the viewer, and switch it to represent the B/W mode.

14 Adjust the Matte finesse controls to cover up any remaining unselected areas.

15 In the 3D qualifier window, click the Invert button to focus the extraction on the plane instead of the water.

16 In the viewer, disable the Highlight mode.

17 In the qualifier palette, deselect Show Paths to hide the selection lines.

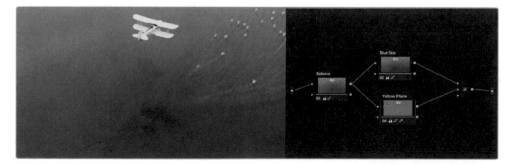

You now have full control over RGB values of the plane.

18   in the adjustment controls of the Color wheel palette, decrease the saturation of the plane.

19   Create a gentle s-curve on the Y channel of the custom curves to enhance the contrast and detail on the plane.

Using Key Inputs and Outputs to Share Matte Data Across Nodes

The key inputs and outputs allow you to reuse node mattes, and further adjust them in the receiving node.

In this example, you have not yet addressed a remaining component of the composite. In the reference video, the flamingos in the upper-right corner of the shot are graded pink. In the current grade, the birds look desaturated and flat. Because you have already keyed-out the green water in the Yellow Plane node, it will be enough to reuse its key data and add a custom curve window to isolate the focus onto the birds in the corner.

1   In clip 08, click the Yellow Plane node.

2   Press Option-L (macOS) or Alt-L (Windows) to create a new Layer node, and label it **Flamingos**.

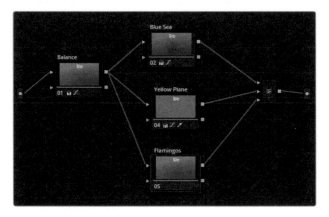

3   To reuse the matte data of the keyed Yellow Plane node, drag the Key output triangle of the plane node toward the key input of the Flamingos node.

By default, when a key is linked to another node, its matte is automatically inverted.

4   Enter the Key palette in the central palettes of the Color page.

5   Next to Key Input, click the Invert button to deselect the automated matte invert.

6   Scrub to the end of the video until you see the area that the flamingos occupy in the frame.

To isolate the matte to include just the birds, use a custom curve window.

7   Open the Window palette, and click the curve window button. Label it **Flamingos Matte**.

8   Click around the flamingos in the image. Remember to click the first point last to close the loop and generate a shape.

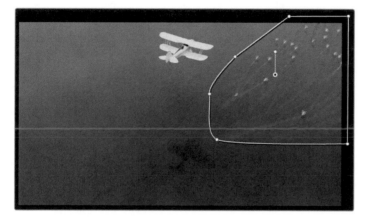

9   The birds appear in the shot only toward the end, so you will perform a rudimentary animation of the window across the screen.

A simple way to animate windows in the Color page is by using the Frame mode of the Tracker palette.

10   Click the diamond-shape in the center of the keyframe controls in the upper-right corner of the tracker graph.

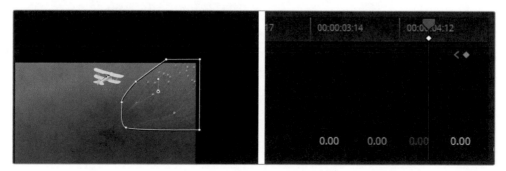

Doing so places the end keyframe for the curve window.

11 Drag the playhead back until the birds are off-screen, and drag the curve window after them in the viewer. The tracker graph automatically places a second keyframe, and an animation is generated between the two.

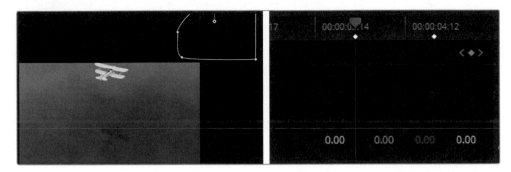

12 Scrub through the clip timeline to ensure the window is following the motion of the birds.

Finally, you can apply the necessary grade adjustments to enhance the pink color of the birds.

13 Drag the Gain master wheel left to darken the birds slightly.

14 Drag the Gain Color Wheel toward magenta to make the birds pink.

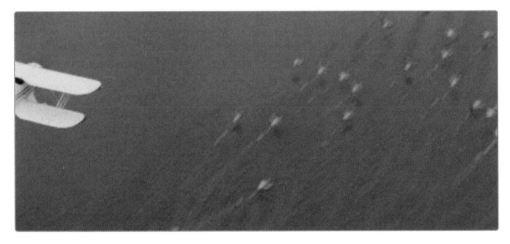

To quickly bypass and evaluate the grade you just created, you can combine all the nodes of the Layer mixer into a single compound node.

15 Drag in the Node editor to select all the nodes except the Balance node.

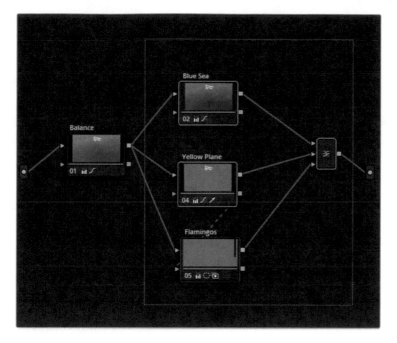

You can press the Cmd-D (macOS) or Ctrl-D (Windows) to bypass the selected nodes without affecting the Balance node.

16 Right-click any selected node, and choose Create Compound Node.

This is an effective organizational tool when working on clips with large node tree structures. Additionally, you can still bypass the node to disable the color composites without affecting the Balance node.

You still have access to the original Layer mixer structure within the Compound node.

17 Right-click and choose Show compound node.

18 To navigate back to the main Node editor, click the project name Project 02 – Age of Airplanes Trailer link at the bottom of the Node editor.

19 If you want to return to the original node structure of the Compound node, right-click, and select Decompose Compound Node.

> **TIP** Another method for decluttering the Node editor is to hide node thumbnails. In the upper-right corner of the Node editor, click the option menu, and denselect Show Thumbnails. Doing so will collapse the nodes to just their labels, numbers, and palette icons.

Importing and using an External Matte

In their natural states, all tools that generate a selection (such as qualifiers and Power Windows) are actually just black-and-white visual guides that tell the image where it needs to be visible (white) and invisible (black). In post-production, these guides are called mattes (or travelling mattes when the matte is animated or generated using keyed live footage). Mattes are seen in the Color page when the viewer is set to Highlight mode and the Highlight B/W option is selected.

Because mattes fundamentally rely on this black-and-white graphic dynamic, any image or video that is black and white can technically be treated as a matte. This could even include outside media imported into Resolve that you can assign to a specific clip for selection purposes.

In this exercise, you will use an externally generated matte for the purpose of targeting and extracting a portion of the image.

1 Click clip 07 on the Airplanes – 01 HQ Timeline.

2 From the "Base grades" album, apply the 1.7.1 Balance grade to the clip to neutralize its starting colors.

Selecting the sky in this image using the standard keying tools is tricky because its elements are visually similar: the sky is almost purely white, together with the snow on the ground, which is reflecting strongly onto the bottom of the airplane.

Using the qualifier alone would not be enough. You would need to generate custom windows need to be generated and track them to create a clean matte composite. Sometimes, this type of advanced keying work is delegated to a rotoscope artist or compositor while the colorist uses her time to focus on grading the media.

In this instance, a matte was already created for this video clip.

3   Enter the Media page.

4   In the Media storage panel, find the BMD 15 CC – Project 02 folder, and navigate to Other > Mattes.

In Mattes, you will find the SOUTH_POLE_MATTE PNG sequence folder. The matte sequence in it will appear as a single video file.

> **NOTE** To import individual stills from image sequences such as PNG or DPX, click the option menu in the upper-right corner of the Media storage panel, and choose Show Individual Frames.

5   Drag SOUTH_POLE_MATTE.png into the Media Pool.

6   Enter the Color page.

7   In the Node editor of clip 07, create a new serial node (node 02) and label it *Sky Removal*.

8   Click the Media pool button at the top of the Color page to open the Media pool panel.

9   From the Graphics bin, drag format SOUTH_POLE_MATTE.png as Media File Name into the Node editor.

The matte PNG sequence appears within a dedicated Ext. Matte node in the Node editor. Notice that the node has no inputs and contains multiple outputs.

The uppermost blue square is the standard luminance, or Y output. The three blue squares under it are RGB outputs that enable you to work on each channel of the image independently. The green square output at the bottom sends a standard RGB signal of the black-and white matte.

10   Drag the uppermost Key output to the Sky Removal node's key input.

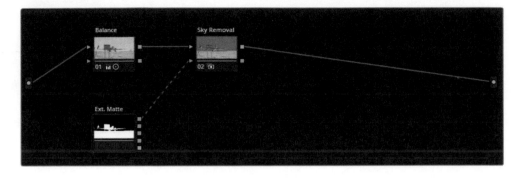

> TIP If the edges of a prerendered matte require expanding or contracting
> (for example if a visible border is around the keyed subject after the matte is
> applied), you can use the Alpha Matte Shrink and Grow FX in the ResolveFX
> Refine section of the OpenFX panel. To be effective, Shrink and Grow must be
> applied to a standard corrector node, and placed between the external matte
> and destination node while connected using standard RGB inputs/outputs.

This workflow is frequently employed when the workload of a composite is broken up
among multiple post-production departments. Though the custom curve window can
be extremely effective for rotoscoping, that activity might not be the best use of a
colorist's time.

Instead, the job could be handed over to a rotoscope or VFX artist who can dedicate
himself to generating an accurate travelling matte using compositing software. When
he is finished, he can export a black-and-white video matte to be shared with the
colorist. She can then use it to quickly extract a key in the Node editor and create the
final grade or shot composite.

Applying Transparency to Multiple Video Tracks

The following exercise will require a basic understanding of editing principles. Specifically,
that a timeline can contain multiple video or audio tracks in which you can stack media to
occupy the same temporal point in the timeline. Ordinarily, clips on upper tracks hide media
on lower tracks, unless transparency is introduced (which could be achieved using effects
such as cropping, opacity reduction, or color blending). The Color page offers more
advanced methods for incorporating transparency into clips and revealing lower video
tracks in the timeline.

1   Right-click in the Node editor, and choose Add Alpha Output.

A new output it added to the Node graph in which you can apply any key data in the
node tree to the alpha channel of the clip.

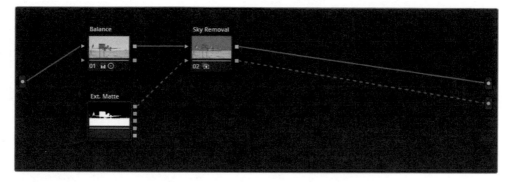

The key data is applied to the clip's alpha channel and affects its appearance in the timeline and upon export. This behavior is different from the way the key data behaves when it is contained within the Node editor. There it can be used only to determine which parts of the image are affected for grading purposes.

3   Enter the Media page.

4   In the Other > Images subfolder of the Media storage, locate the Sky_Stock.jpg file, and drag it into the Media pool's Graphics bin.

If the sky image's colors appear distorted in the viewer, it is because they are impacted by the color management of the project.

5   In the Media pool, right-click the image thumbnail, and choose Input Color space > Bypass.

6   Enter the Edit page.

7   Drag the zoom slider, or press Cmd-+ (plus sign) in macOS or Ctrl-+ (plus sign) in Windows, to zoom in on the SOUTH_POLE clip.

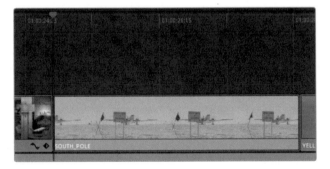

8   Drag the clip to video track 2. Doing so will create an empty space on the video track underneath.

9   With the clip still selected, press the X key to create an in/out selection equal to the clip's duration.

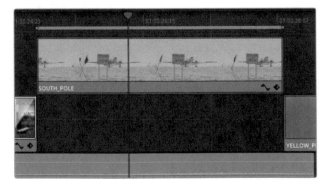

10 Drag Sky_Stock.jpg from the Media pool into the timeline viewer. When the viewer's
edit controls appear, drag the image into Fit to Fill.

This action will fill the gap under the airplane clip with the still image of the sky based
on the earlier in/out selection.

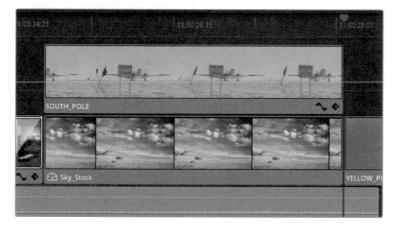

The end result will be a rough composite of the two images.

Image Processing Cross DaVinci Resolve Pages

The layout of the pages at the bottom of the DaVinci Resolve interface represents the project workflow. Media is ingested (Media page), compiled into a timeline (Edit page), undergoes compositing (Fusion page), and is then graded (Color page) and mixed (Fairlight page) before being rendered (Deliver page).

This order of operations also corresponds to the image-processing pipeline with some distinctions. The video signal of the source media in the Edit page flows to the Fusion page, where it is processed and output to the Color page. However, if an effect (ResolveFX or OFX plug-in) is applied in the Edit page, it will NOT appear in the Fusion page, but will appear on the Color page. It is helpful to think of Edit page effects as being applied to the image data signal after it has left the Fusion page. To force an Edit page effect to become visible in the Fusion page, you would need to turn the clip into a compound clip on the timeline.

Finally, the viewers on all three pages represent different stages of the video signal. The Edit page has two viewers: the Source viewer shows the ungraded source video signal; the Timeline viewer shows the signal after it has been processed by both the Fusion and Color pages. The Fusion page shows the ungraded video signal of a source or compound clip. The Color page shows all Edit and Fusion page effects, as well as the grading information.

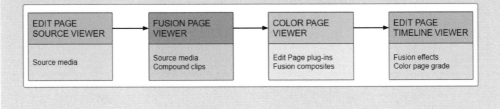

Your next step is to clean up placement, colors, and keys of both layers.

1 Enter the Color page.

> **TIP** If the sky is not visible behind the plane in the viewer, click the Unmix button in the lower-left of the viewer to activate the composited view.

2 In the timeline, select the Sky_Stock image clip.

3 Open the Sizing palette, and adjust the Pan, Tilt, and Zoom values to fill the background with the sky image.

4 Select the SOUTH_POLE clip (now identified in the timeline as clip 08).

Playing through the footage, you will find that the matte does not appear to be in time with the video. Mattes often includes handles to facilitate small trims. Other times, there is just an offset of 1-2 frames.

5 With the Ext. Matte node selected in the Node editor, open the Key palette. The controls at the bottom allow you to modify the position of a matte with multiple frames.

6 Deselect Loop and Lock Matte to prevent the travelling matte from looping. Doing so will also allow you to offset when it begins and ends.

7 Drag or type the Offset value to **1** (frame) to fix the alignment. The matte will now match the airplane clip.

Next, you will match the colors of the two layers to create a single neutral look for the environment.

8 Create a serial node after the Sky Removal node, and label it Sky Match. This node does not need to interfere with the Key output of the Sky Removal node, which continues to carry the necessary transparency data to the node tree output.

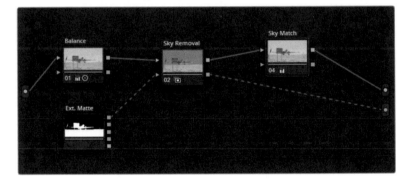

9 In the adjustment controls, increase the Contrast of the SOUTH_POLE plane footage, and drag the Offset wheel toward blue to cool it down.

You can make the sky look more realistic by blending it into the original video slightly. For that, you will need to adjust the matte key.

10 Click the Sky Removal node.

11 In the Key palette, drag the Key Input Offset to the right (0.300) to reintroduce some of the original sky into the composite.

Performing a Match Move

Finally, you can match the movement of the sky to the pan of the camera in the plane shot.

1   With the Sky Match node selected, open the Window palette.

2   Create a circle window and place it over the sign in the foreground to limit your grade to just the sign area; however, it is only a temporary window necessary for performing a track. You will disable it after the track data is extracted.

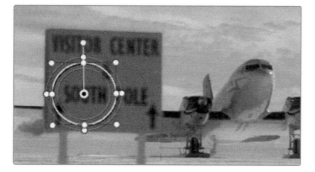

3   Open the Tracker palette.

4   At the top, deselect the Zoom, Rotate, and 3D parameters. This clip requires only a smooth track of the pan and tilt, and three-dimensional parameters will most likely interfere with the result.

5   Click analyze forward to perform a track of the camera pan.

6   When the track is complete, open the Tracker options menu in the upper-right of the palette, and choose Copy Track Data.

7   Go back to the Window palette, and click the circle button to disable it. The grade returns to the rest of your image and you now have the track data that you need to apply to the sky.

8   In the timeline, click the Sky_Stock image clip.

9   Open the Tracker palette, and change the mode to Stabilizer.

10 In the options menu of the Tracker palette, choose Classic Stabilizer. Doing so will give you access to the Smooth and Strong controls of the stabilizer, which are necessary for match moving.

11 Click the options menu of the Tracker palette again, and choose Paste Track Data.

    You should see the tracker graph fill up with the transform controls from the SOUTH_POLE clip track that you just generated and copied.

12   At the bottom of the palette, set Strong to -100 to invert the track data and apply it to the sky image, thereby creating the illusion of the sky moving with the foreground.

13   In the upper-right of the palette, click Stabilize to apply the tracking data. The sky is now tracked to the foreground image.

> **TIP** You can enter a Strong value of -95 to slightly offset the track on the background image, resulting in a more natural-looking parallax effect.

With the composite cleaned up, you can combine the two layers to continue treating them as a single clip.

14   Enter the Edit page.

15   Select both the SOUTH_POLE clip and the sky image underneath it.

16   Right-click either clip, and choose New Compound Clip. Name it **South Pole**.

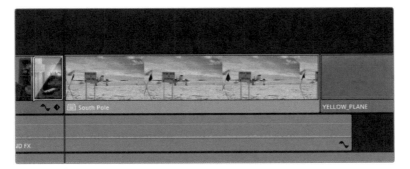

> **NOTE** Right-clicking a clip in the timeline will also allow you to choose New Fusion Connect Clip. This choice will launch Blackmagic Design's Fusion compositing software and allow you to assemble your image in a dedicated node-based compositing software. The link between the media will be live, and any changes applied in Fusion will translate to the clip in the Resolve timeline.

17 Enter the Color page.

The South Pole clip has a blank Node editor into which you can start applying a binding grade to make the composite truly look like a real image.

18 Label the current node Look, and tweak the colors to give the composite a colorful cyan look.

19 Create a second node called Vignette, and apply a vignette around the image.

> **TIP** The two composited layers are still accessible by right-clicking the compound clip in the Edit page, and choosing Open in Timeline.

While extracting a portion of an image based on qualifier keys or mattes is generally straightforward, the real challenge is in assessing the end result and determining what you must do to achieve a realistic composite. It is helpful to write out a list of everything that looks unconvincing in the constructed image and address each item one at a time: shadows, color match, scaling, positioning, and so on.

The exercises in this lesson were designed to give you an overview of the potential of the Node editor. Though you've practiced a variety of possible workflows, there is ultimately no single correct way to utilize nodes in grading. Continue to practice using nodes for more advanced grading and you will soon arrive at your own preferred style. Above all, aim for the dual goals of workflow efficiency and the preservation of image quality.

Self-guided Exercise

Complete the following exercises in the Airplanes – 01 HQ Timeline to test your understanding of the tools and workflows covered in this lesson.

Clip 05 - Find the external matte for this clip in the Project 02 – Age of Airplanes Trailer folder, and use it to retain the color of the poster in the background while making the rest of the image black and white.

When finished, combine the background and poster nodes via a Layer mixer node and experiment with the blending modes to find more dramatic or subtle ways of integrating the colors of the poster into the black-and-white image.

When you've completed this exercise, you can open and view the Project 02 – Age of Airplanes Trailer COMPLETED.drp to compare your node construction on this clip with a finished version of the project.

Lesson Review

1   Can a corrector node have multiple RGB inputs?

2   What are the blue symbols on either side of a node?

3   True or False? A node key can be connected to the input of a node that is in the same parallel or layer mixer stack.

4   In the Key palette, what does the Key Output Gain affect?

5   True or False? You can add additional RGB inputs to mixer nodes.

Answers

1   No. A corrector node can only have a single RGB input, though it can have multiple RGB (and key) outputs.

2   Key input and output.

3   True. A node output (both RGB and key) can be linked to any other input further down the pipeline, as well as to other nodes in a mixer stack.

4   Opacity of the selected node.

5   True. Right-click a mixer node to add more inputs.

Managing Grades Across Clips and Timelines

Grading a film or video project requires a considerable level of attention to detail and the use of a variety of tools throughout both primary and secondary stages. However, once a look is established, a project often makes repeated use of existing grades that propagate throughout the timeline. An obvious example of this is when you are working on multiple clips that come from the same source file, or clips used from different takes of the same shot.

DaVinci Resolve 15 includes a wide variety of workflows that help reproduce and refine grades across clips. These include the straightforward copy and paste, the extraction of individual nodes for isolated adjustments, and even the migration of grades across different timelines. The aim of this lesson is to introduce you to the variety of workflows you will need to efficiently copy and manage grades within a project and beyond.

Time

This lesson takes approximately 45 minutes to complete.

Goals

Working with Local Versions

Versions enable you to associate multiple grades with a single clip in a timeline. You can use versions to preserve a grade at earlier stages of the grading process, or when creating a series of shot-grading options to share with a creative supervisor for selection and approval. Each version will remain intact and can be recalled when needed. Versions are easily accessible in the contextual menu of each clip and can be created, deleted, bypassed, and switched between local and remote.

In this exercise, you will begin with creating a new grade on a clip, and then apply preexisting grades from the gallery to quickly build up a set of local versions.

1   Open Project 02 - Age of Airplanes Trailer.

2   Enter the Color page.

3   In the Airplanes - 01 HQ Timeline, click clip 04.

4   For a better representation of the clip's content, drag the playhead to the middle of the clip where the plane is in view.

5   Open the Base grades album, right-click the 1.4.1. Balance still, and choose Apply Grade.

> **NOTE** The numbers under the stills reference the timeline track, the clip number, and the number of stills generated for that clip.

6   Create a second node on clip 04 labelled Cross Process.

7   Open the custom curves palette. To create a cross-process look, you will want to push opposing complementary colors into the image highlights and shadows. This tends to result in a retro film camera look.

8   Click the YRGB link to ungang the channels.

9   Isolate the blue channel, and drag the black point up to turn the shadows blue. Then drag its white point down to turn the highlights yellow.

10 Isolate the red channel, and create control points in its lower and upper midtones. Drag them into an s-curve, thereby pushing cyan into the shadows and red into the highlights.

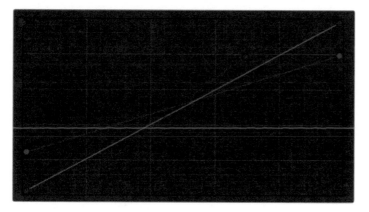

11 Create a new serial node 03 and label it Contrast.

12 In the adjustment controls of the Color wheel palette, increase the contrast of the image (1.200) and use the pivot to reduce the strong exposure in the sky (0.600).

You have now successfully created the first look for this shot. By default, every clip begins with a Local Version 1. You can rename the version to identify a specific look or purpose of a grade.

13 In the timeline, right click the clip 04 thumbnail, and choose Version 1 > Rename.

14 Enter the name **Cross process**, and click OK.

You will be applying several variants of grades on this clip. Each variant with will be designated as a new local version. To save time, you will use the preexisting grades in the Clip 04 grades album of the gallery.

15 Right-click clip 04, and choose Local Versions > Create New Version. Enter the name **Bleach bypass**.

16 Reset the cross process grade by choosing Color > Reset All Grades and Nodes.

This is a necessary step if you want to start with a fresh clip every time you design a new look. Otherwise, you can continue tweaking the image using the previous grade's settings.

> **NOTE** The fastest way to copy grade data between stills and grades is by using the middle button of your mouse. Select the clip you want to grade and center-click a still in the gallery or a clip in the timeline to copy its grade.

17 In the Clip 04 grades album, middle-click the Bleach bypass still to apply the grade.

> **TIP** If your mouse does not have a middle button, right-click a still, or any clip on the timeline to open the contextual menu, and choose Apply Grade to copy the grade to the currently selected clip.

18 To make another version, right-click the clip again, and choose Local Versions > Create New Version. Enter the name **Simple pop**.

You could reset the grade again, but because you are simply overwriting the current grade with the still grade, that will not be necessary.

19 In the Clip 04 grades album, middle-click the Simple Pop still to apply the grade.

> **TIP** Press Cmd-Y (macOS) or Ctrl-Y (Windows) to create a new version in a clip.

20 Right-click clip 04, and choose Local Versions > Create New Version. Enter the name Navy blue.

21 In the Clip 04 grades album, middle-click the Navy blue still to apply the grade.

Having created a series of versions, you can now compare them in the viewer using a split-screen display.

22 At the top of the viewer, between the Image Wipe and Highlight buttons, click the Split Screen button.

23 In the upper-right corner of the viewer, choose Version.

The split-screen view is enabled, displaying all four grades in a grid in the viewer.

Comparing the versions might be difficult at the moment because they have been scaled-down to fit into the small viewer window. You can resize the viewer for full-screen playback and optimal viewing.

24 Choose Workspace > Viewer Mode > Cinema Viewer, or press Cmd-F (macOS) or Ctrl-F (Windows).

In the next few exercises, you will apply the cross process look to other clips in the timeline.

25 Double-click the Cross process version in the upper-left corner of the split-screen view to select it.

26 Press Esc to exit the full-screen mode.

27 Right-click in the viewer, and choose Split Screen > On/Off to disable the split-screen view, or click the Split Screen button above the viewer.

> **TIP** Press Cmd-B or Cmd-N (macOS), or Ctrl-B or Ctrl-N (Windows) to cycle through the versions of a clip in the viewer.

Remote Versions

In the contextual menu, under the Local Versions options, you may have noticed a similar section for remote versions. This area offers another method of retaining multiple grades in a clip.

Remote versions are different from local versions in two ways: first, when a clip is graded within a remote version, its grade affects all other timeline clips that were derived from the same source clip; and second, the grade appears on all subsequent uses of the source clip in all other timelines of the active project (provided that the clips in those timelines are also using remote versions).

One popular application for remote version grading is for a DIT (digital imaging technician) using master timeline workflows. Upon ingesting, you can place all the media on a remote timeline and apply preliminary grading to the clips. When you eventually create a cut in the Edit page, or migrate an editor's timeline, those remote grades will automatically transfer to the new timeline, provided that the clips in the new timeline are all using remote versions. In short, local version grades are applied on a timeline basis, whereas remote versions are applied on a project basis.

Appending Grades and Nodes

In the previous exercise, you applied stills grades onto a clip by choosing the Apply Grade contextual menu option in the stills, or pressing the middle button of your mouse. This overwrites the existing grade on a clip and replaces it with the entire node tree of the copied grade. There will often be times when you will want to apply just portions of a node tree, or add the node tree after a clip has undergone balancing or matching.

The following exercises will show you how to be selective with copying grade nodes.

1 Click clip 02 on Airplanes – 01 HQ Timeline. You will be applying the cross process grade onto this clip.

Clip 02 is currently unbalanced and has a strong yellow tint. You could normalize and balance it, but that would not necessarily optimize it for the cross process grade. As was emphasized in Lesson 2, clips need to be matched to share grade data accurately. Without matching, grades will behave unpredictably and the differences between the clips will continue to be obvious.

A match has been prepared for this exercise.

2   Open the "Base grades" album, and apply the 1.2.1. Match still to the clip. To more closely match 04, the highlights were neutralized, and the contrast softened.

3   Open the "Clip 04" grades album.

A cross process grade was already prepared and stored in the gallery. If you directly apply the cross process still from the gallery, it will overwrite the base grade you just applied to the clip. Instead, you will append the cross process grade to the matched Node graph.

4   Right-click the 1.4.1 Cross process still, and choose Append Node graph.

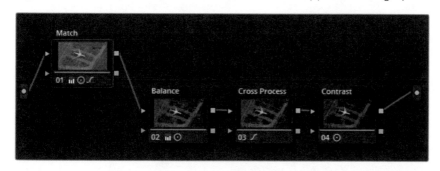

> **TIP** You can also drag a still from the gallery onto a connection line in the Node graph to append it to an existing grade.

Clip 02 now has a match node, followed by the cross process. However, the grade still does not look right. By appending the grade, you added all the nodes from that version, included the original Balance node that was created specifically for clip 04. That node does not work in the context of clip 02 and should be deleted.

5   Select node 02 Balance, and press the Delete or Backspace key on the keyboard.

You now have a clean cross-process look on the second airplane shot that more closely resembles the one in clip 04. You'll apply this same look to a third shot, this time without the Balance or Contrast nodes.

Copying Individual Nodes from a Still

So far, you have been using the grading data stored within stills in its entirety. You copied and appended the entire node pipeline to the Node editor, and tweaked the nodes based on the clip needs.

However, you also have access to a still's Node graph while it is still in the gallery. This allows you to apply very specific adjustments from a saved grade.

1   Click clip 03 on Airplanes – 01 HQ Timeline.

This clip looks relatively neutral but is distinctly different from the starting looks of clips 02 and 04. As in the previous exercise, you will apply a match still to prepare it for the cross process look.

2 Open the "Base grades" album, and apply the 1.3.1. Match and Contrast still to the clip.

Doing so significantly alters the look of the clip but is vital for ensuring a good base for the incoming grade. The Match node is there to mimic the yellow tint of clip 02, while the Contrast node addresses the stark difference in location and shot angle to more closely match the final luminance ranges of clips 02 and 04.

You can proceed to apply the cross process grade. Because the clip is balanced and already has contrast, you need only to transfer the cross process node itself.

3 Open the "Clip 04 grades" album, right-click the 1.4.1 Cross process still, and choose Display Node graph.

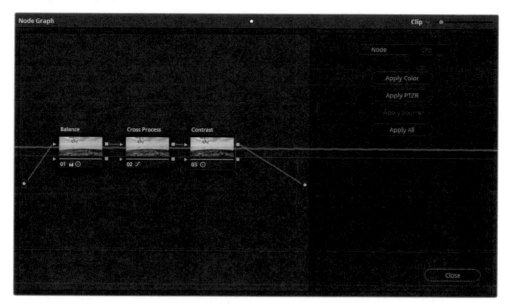

The Node graph appears in a separate window, with the node pipeline of the still and a series of controls over how and what you want copied.

To the right side of the window is a tabbed interface that allows you to apply only the color adjustments or only the sizing adjustments of the Node graph (PTZR — pan, tilt, zoom, rotation).

A button at the top allows you to switch to a node-based refinement of the parameters that will be included during copying.

4 From the still's Node graph window, drag node 02, Color Process, to the Node editor of clip 03. Hover it over to the connection link between node 01, Match, and node 02, Contrast.

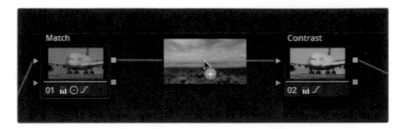

A + (plus sign) will appear over the link to signify that you can release the mouse and attach the Color Process node between Match and Contrast.

5   In the still's Node graph window, click Close.

Having access to the node structure of every still facilitates cleaner, more precise workflows. You separate the primary balance and match nodes from the contrast and creative look nodes and only copy what is necessary for every new clip grade. As with all grading, you should to tweak and refine the grades to ensure maximum visual quality and similarity.

Using Shared Nodes Across Multiple Clips

As mentioned previously, color grading is often an iterative process. After establishing an initial grade, you will often return to earlier nodes to make additional tweaks. When unifying a look across multiple clips, these minor adjustments can become extremely time consuming as you manually copy node data between clips, each with individual node structures.

DaVinci Resolve provides several tools and techniques to simplify this tweaking process as much as possible. Amongst those tools are Shared nodes, which allow you to link and lock a single node across multiple clips. In this exercise, you will create a Shared node across three clips and change their collective look with a single adjustment.

1   Click clip 02 on the Airplanes – 01 HQ Timeline.

2   In the Node editor, right-click node 02 Cross Process, and choose Save as Shared Node.

The node now features a pair of blue arrows to indicate its status as a Shared node. Additionally, an icon in the lower-right corner shows that the node is locked.

3   By default, the node is renamed to Shared Node 1. Right-click and choose Node Label to rename the node to Cross Look.

Before making changes to this grade, let's assign the shared node to clips 03 and 04.

4   Click clip 03.

5   In the Node editor, right-click node 02 Cross Process, and choose Add Node > Cross Look.

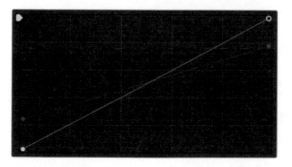

The Cross Look shared node is added after node 03, thereby doubling the effect of the cross process grade.

6   Select node 03 Cross Process, and press Backspace to remove it.

7   Click clip 04, and repeat steps 5 and 6 to replace its existing cross process node with the shared node. The three clips now share the Cross Look node.

8   While still on clip 04, right-click the shared node (03 Cross Look), and choose Lock Node to disable the lock.

9   In the custom curves palette, ensure that the channels are unganged.

10 Isolate the red channel, and reverse its S-curve by dragging up the lower midtone point, and dragging down the upper midtone point.

Doing so has the effect of flipping the colors used in the cross process look, while still maintaining a similar retro film appearance.

11 Click clips 02 and 03 to verify that the adjustment was copied to these clips.

12   Right-click the shared node on any of the clips, and choose Lock Node to prevent accidental changes.

Let's now add a vignette to a new node on all three clips.

13   In the Node editor, select the last node on clip 02, and press Option-S (macOS) or Alt-S (Windows) to add a fourth node.

14   Right-click node 04, and choose Save as Shared Node.

15   Label node 04 as **Vignette**, and unlock it.

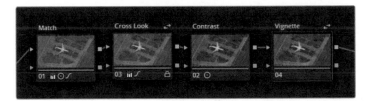

16   Open the Window palette. Instead of creating a new vignette from scratch, you can reuse the preset you generated in the previous project.

17   In the upper-right corner, in the option menu, choose the Vignette preset.

18   Drag the resulting vignette circle over the center of the frame, and in the viewer, expand its size.

19   Drag down the Gamma master wheel to darken the edges of the frame.

20   With clip 02 still selected in the timeline, Shift-click clip 04 to select clips 02, 03, and 04 sequentially. The selection is indicated by a red highlight in the timeline.

21 Choose Color > Append Node to Selected Clips.

Doing so adds the selected node to the end of the pipeline of all selected clips on the timeline. This action is often used to copy a look across multiple clips, but it can be even more effective when appending a shared node, which you can continue to use for future adjustments.

Shared nodes behave similarly to regular Corrector nodes, which makes them easy to use across a variety of grading and organizational workflows. You can copy and paste shared nodes using keyboard shortcuts, retain them when switching between versions, and even save them in the pipelines of Gallery stills.

TIP You can create an ungraded (but fully labelled) node pipeline and save it as a still to use as a preset for future grades. Shared nodes can be preemptively included in preset pipelines to ensure that creative grades are automatically applied across all clips when grading.

Saving Grades for other Projects

The stills contained in the gallery albums of the Color page will ordinarily be accessible only in the project they are contained in. A different kind of gallery album, the PowerGrade, makes stills accessible to all other projects generated by the same user (and within the same database) on a workstation.

1 In the Albums list of the gallery, open the "Clip 04 grades" album.

2 Drag the Bleach bypass still to the PowerGrade 1 album at the bottom of the list.

3 Click the PowerGrade 1 album to view its contents. The Bleach bypass now appears in the PowerGrade 1 album of all the projects you create on your current workstation.

The gallery panel also has additional features contained in its expanded version.

4 In the upper-right corner of the gallery, click the gallery view button.

A separate window opens displaying the full contents of the gallery.

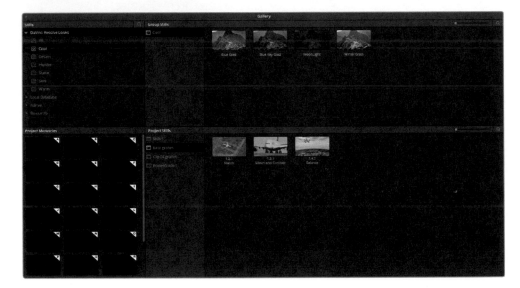

The Stills panel in the upper-left features a collection of DaVinci Resolve looks and provides access to stills from other databases and projects on the same workstation. The Group Stills panel next to it displays the stills associated with the album that is currently selected.

At the bottom is the current project's gallery panel, and to its left is the Project Memories panel, which enables you to designate shortcuts to frequently used stills.

> **TIP** To save a still as a memory, drag it from the gallery onto one of the memory slots. You can apply these memories to clips on the timeline using shortcuts that correspond to the letter of the memory as expressed numerically. For example, memory B will have the shortcut Cmd-2 (macOS) or Ctrl-2 (Windows).

5   In the lower-half of the full gallery window, select the PowerGrade 1 album.

6   In the DaVinci Resolve Looks list, select the Hipster album, and drag the **Crossed Dye** still in the Powergrade album, into the Project Stills window below.

You've now moved one of the preset stills into the gallery and will be able to apply it to the current project.

7   Close the gallery view.

8   In Airplanes – 01 HQ Timeline, choose clip 07.

9   Right-click and create a new local version called **Crossed Dye**.

10 Right-click the **Crossed Dye** still, and choose Apply Grade.

> **TIP** You can double-click a PowerGrade still to apply the grade to a selected clip on the timeline.

Outside of using databases and PowerGrade albums, you can also share grades across different workstations by exporting them from the gallery.

11 In the gallery, open the Clip 04 grades album, and right-click the 1.4.1. Cross process still.

12 In the pop-up menu, choose Export.

The still's visual and grading information is exported and contained in two files. The DPX file format is an image format used for comparison and review. The DRX file contains the node tree and grading data. You need both files to be able to migrate stills with grade information.

13 Indicate a location on your workstation, create a folder for the two files, and label it Airport cross process. Confirm by clicking Export.

14 Open a file browser on your computer and locate the two files.

The DPX file can be shared like any regular image file without the need for Resolve. The DRX file is a DaVinci Resolve exchange file used to carry the grading parameters for the shot and can only be used together with the DPX. To import a grade into a new Resolve project, both files must be located in the same folder or directory.

15 Return to the Color page, and in the gallery, open the PowerGrade 1 album.

16 Right-click and choose Import.

17 In the file browser, locate the BMD 15 CC – Project 02 folder, and navigate to Other > Stills.

18 Select Punchy film_1.9.1.dpx, and click Import.

Note that only the DPX file is visible in the Resolve file browser, even though the DRX file is located in the same folder. The DRX file is bound to the DPX and its grading data will be included in the still upon import.

19 Apply the "Punchy film" grade to clip 09 in the timeline.

NOTE Selecting the "Export with Display LUT" option will export the DPX and DRX files in a format that is supported by monitoring applications. You can upload these files to camera viewers or monitor displays.

Here are some additional options for working with the Gallery and stills that many colorists employ for organizational and practical purposes:

- **Right-click in the viewer, and choose Grab All Stills**. Doing so will generate a still for each clip in the timeline (either from the first or middle frame) and placed them in the Media pool. Colorists use this option to keep track of their grade process and separate the stills into pass bins (balance, match, secondary, and so on).

- **Right-click in the gallery, and choose One Still Per Scene**. This choice will restrict the number of stills you generate from any given clip to just one still. This is a popular option for colorists who frequently grab stills of their clips while grading, and do not want the gallery to become cluttered with thumbnails.

Copying Timeline Grades using ColorTrace

ColorTrace is a feature in DaVinci Resolve that enables the transfer of grading information from one timeline to another. It is a much faster and more organized method of copying mass grade data than using stills.

One scenario in which ColorTrace may be used is when multiple project types use the same source materials (film, trailer, teaser, behind-the-scenes, and do on). Another scenario is when an editor creates changes in a timeline that a colorist has already begun grading. In both cases, a major task would usually await the colorist: a still would need to be created for each clip in the timeline and then carefully reapplied to each corresponding clip on the new timeline. This job has the potential for many issues because an overworked colorist might have to generate and organize dozens (or hundreds) of stills in the Gallery.

ColorTrace bypasses all that by presenting two timelines side-by-side and helping the colorist identify where their common media is located. The colorist then needs only to confirm (or deny) that the media is correct, and the transference of grading data is instantaneous.

1   Enter the Edit page, and in the Media pool, open the Timelines bin.

2   Choose File > Import Timeline > Import AAF, EDL, XML.

3   Navigate to the Project 02 – Age of Airplanes Trailer folder, open the XML subfolder, and select Airplane – 02 Color trace.xml. Click Open to import it.

4   In the Load XML window, deselect the option to Automatically import source clips into Media pool, and click Ok.

A pop up will prompt you to indicate the bins where the timeline's media is contained.

5   Expand the bin structure, and deselect the LQ Transcodes bin to ensure the media is linked only to the high quality versions of the clips. Click Ok.

> **NOTE** If any media does not appear on the timeline, it is possible that the corresponding HQ clip is not in the Media pool. Into the Media page, and drag any remaining clips from the Media storage HQ transcodes folder into the Media pool HQ bin.

The Airplane - 02 Color trace edit will appear in the timeline panel of the Edit page.

6   Enter the Color page to check the grade status of the clips.

None of the grades applied to the Airplanes – 01 HQ Timeline have been transferred.

7   Return to the Edit page.

8   In the Media pool, right-click the Airplane – 02 Color trace timeline, and choose Timelines > ColorTrace > ColorTrace from Timeline.

9   In the ColorTrace Setup window, expand the Local Database folder and locate Airplanes – 01 HQ Timeline.

Effects and Definitions

The Effects and Definitions panel underneath the Project List enables you to define a set of naming conventions for clips in the timeline with names that were changed since the original timeline versions.

An example is applying this feature in VFX workflows. Assume that the original filenames of two timeline clips were **car.mov** and **sky.mov**. Both clips were sent to the VFX department for some compositing work. The VFX department returns the finished composites under the names **car_vfx.mov** and **sky_vfx.mov**, and they are inserted into a new version of the timeline. When ColorTrace is used to transfer the grading data from the original timeline, the two VFX clips are not recognized due to their new filenames. By entering ***_vfx** in the Effects and Definitions panel, Resolve can exempt the suffix when associating the media between the timelines.

10 Select the timeline and click Continue to proceed to the ColorTrace interface.

At the top of the interface, you'll find options to switch between the Automatic and Manual modes of the feature.

Automatic attempts to locate the same clips used in both timelines based on source name, regardless of change in position or trim.

Manual allows you to identify matched clips by selecting them yourself. With this method, you can assign grades when the original filenames or metadata has changed between edits.

The bottom of the interface provides additional information and control over the copy parameters. To the left is a table that compares the metadata of the source and target clips, which is useful when comparing the file paths of two clips to ensure that they are derived from the same take. To the right is a list of criteria that will be included or removed during the grade transfer.

The clips in the Target Timeline have colored outlines that indicate the grade match status of the clips:

- **Red** - No match was found.
- **Blue** - Multiple potential matches were found.
- **Green** - A match was found.

You will need to review the Target Timeline to ensure that the matches are accurate.

> **TIP** Select Hide Matched Clips at the bottom of the interface to remove all clips that have already been matched in the timeline. Doing so will allow you to focus on the clips with no matches or conflicting matches.

11 Clip 01 on the Target Timeline has a blue outline. Select it to see which clips are proposed as possible options in the Matching Source Clips list above it.

Clip 01 clearly corresponds to the clip numbered as 09 in the source clips window.

12 Double-click clip 09 to confirm the match. Both clips' outlines will turn magenta to confirm the selection.

13 Clip 02 also has a blue outline. Select it, and double-click the corresponding clip 08 above to confirm the correct match.

14 Clip 03 has a red outline and offers no options in the Matching Source Clips list. You will address this clip manually after confirming the automatic matches first.

> **NOTE** You can use Set As New Shot to identify clips with no links to the original timeline. They will appear ungraded after the ColorTrace is performed.

15 Clip 06 has a blue outline. Click it to reveal two identical-looking clips.

Check the metadata in the lower-left columns to verify that both clips come from the same source. The REC timecode of source clip 06 is nearer to the timecode of the target clip. Usually, this implies that the same trimmed media is in different versions of an edit.

16 Double-click clip 06 in the source timeline. Both the source and timeline clip outlines should turn magenta.

17 At the bottom of the window, click Copy Grade to confirm the copying of grade data between the green and magenta clips.

18 To resolve the red clips, click the Manual tab at the top of the window.

19 Select clip 03 in the Target Timeline.

The source Timeline does not feature this clip. However, it is extremely similar to clip 02, which features a wider version of the same shot.

20 In the source timeline, select clip 02, and click Paste to confirm the grade transfer.

21 Select clip 07 in the target timeline and manually paste the grade from clip 07 of the source timeline.

22 Click Done, and exit the ColorTrace interface.

23 Enter the Color page to verify that all the clips that were graded in the 01 HQ Timeline were successfully copied to the 02 Color trace timeline.

Just as migrating timelines requires confirmation, the ColorTrace function also calls for some manual review to ensure all grades have transferred correctly. Regardless, it still substantially reduces your workload by managing the majority of the color transference.

Copying Grades using the Timelines Album

One of the quickest ways to transfer a grade between clips in different timelines is by using the Timelines albums in the Gallery.

In the previous exercise, two clips in the Airplanes – 02 Color trace timeline remained ungraded because their counterparts in the 01 HQ Transcodes timelines were also ungraded. In this exercise, you will perform a quick grade on both clips and transfer the grades to the original timeline.

1 In the Airplanes – 02 Color trace Timeline, click clip 06.

2 Use the master wheels to increase contrast in the interview clip, and then adjust the Temp (in page 2 of the Adjustment Controls) to give the image a warm look.

Before

After

3 In the Airplanes – 02 Color trace Timeline, click clip 08.

4 In the custom curves palette, ungang the channels, and adjust the Y curve to increase the contrast in the night time-lapse footage.

5 Switch to the red channel, and create an S-curve to add cyan to the lower midtones of the image.

Before

After

6 Use the pop-up menu above the viewer to return to the Airplanes – 01 HQ Transcodes Timeline.

7   In the gallery panel, click the Timelines album.

8   Use the upper pop-up menu to switch the gallery to the Airplanes – 02 Color trace Timeline stills.

The gallery now displays the current state of all the clips in the 02 Color trace timeline. Note that even the ungraded credits clip is included. This behavior helps you keep track of both graded and ungraded clips in various timelines.

9   In the Airplanes – 01 HQ Transcodes Timeline, select clip 06.

10 In the gallery, right-click clip 06, and choose Apply Grade to transfer the warm interview look across.

11 In the Airplanes – 01 HQ Transcodes Timeline, select clip 10.

12 In the gallery, right-click clip 08, and choose Apply Grade.

All the clips in the Airplanes – 01 HQ Transcodes Timeline are now graded.

The exercises in this lesson presented a broader list of options for grade setup and duplication. When copying grade data, it is important to consider your needs on a project-by-project basis. In most cases, a combination of one or more of these copying methods is ideal; in other cases, a mix of methods could be less efficient than employing a more broad-based solution such as remote versions or ColorTrace.

Lesson Review

1   How do you create new local version of a grade?

2   Which shortcut resets the entire grade of a clip?

3   Where can you access stills saved in other projects and databases on the workstation?

4   What would you do to copy across just one node from the node tree of a still in the gallery?

5   Yes or no? It is possible to appoint shortcuts to your favourite grades and stills.

Answers

1   Right-click and choose Local Versions > Create New Version, or press Cmd-Y (macOs) or Ctrl-Y (Windows).

2   Cmd-Home (macOs) or Ctrl-Home (Windows).

3   Click the Gallery View button to access the expanded gallery.

4   Right-click the still and select Display Node Graph; then drag the relevant node into the node editor of the active clip.

5   Yes, in the form of project Memories.

Part 3: Optimizing the Grading Workflow

Lessons

- Adjusting Image Properties
- Using Groups in the Grading Workflow
- Working with RAW media
- Project Delivery

Welcome to Part III of DaVinci Resolve 15: Color correction Beyond the Basics. This section covers even more advanced node-based grading workflows and looks under the hood of the many processes within Resolve that manipulate and render the image data. As usual, the emphasis will be on image-processing efficiency as you learn to set up RAW materials, adopt grouping grading workflows, and deliver the final project.

> **Project File Location**
>
> You will find all the necessary content for this section in the corresponding folder BMD 15 CC - Project 03. Continue to follow the instructions at the start of every lesson to find the necessary folder, project and timeline. If you have not downloaded the third set of content files, return to the Getting Started section in this book for more information.

Adjusting Image Properties

Though the colors of an image tend to be a primary concern of the colorist, many transformative changes can be made to footage to better accommodate the narrative and aesthetic output of a project. Such changes could include physical alterations to the scaling and positioning of the frame, noise reduction, and keyframing grades to change over time.

Applying such changes can impact the speed at which your computer is able to render and play back the clips. For this reason, it is also helpful to know how to leverage the multiple caching methods in Resolve to ensure the quickest render on a clip and node basis, using both automatic (smart) and manual (user) methods.

Time

This lesson takes approximately 90 minutes to complete.

Goals

Preparing Media using Scene Cut Detection

Your final video project in this book involves a single self-contained video file. Placing the video file directly into a timeline in DaVinci Resolve 15 would result in it being treated as one clip with all grading changes affecting it uniformly. To avoid this, you first need to place cuts throughout the timeline to separate the individual shots and allow for content-specific grading. Doing this manually is time-consuming detail work.

Fortunately, the scene cut detection feature in Resolve performs the heavy lifting for you. It can analyze edited video files prior to import to break up their content into subclips and allow for clip-by-clip grading.

1   Open DaVinci Resolve 15.

2   In the Project manager, click the new project button, and enter the name **Project 03 - The Long Work Day Commercial**.

3   Right-click in the bin list next to the Media pool and choose Add Bin. Label this new bin, Video.

4   In the Media storage library of the Media page, locate the BMD 15 CC - Project 03 folder.

5   In the folder, right-click the Project 03 - The Long Work Day SCD.mov file, and choose Scene Cut Detection.

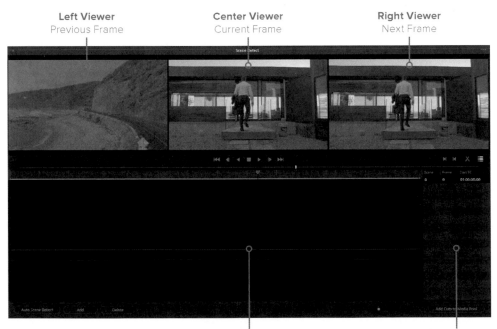

Left Viewer — Previous Frame   Center Viewer — Current Frame   Right Viewer — Next Frame

Scene Detect graph   Cut List

The Scene Detect window appears. You will use this interface to run the edit analysis and import the resulting subclips. At the top of the window are three viewers that display the current frame (middle); the previous frame (left), and the following frame (right). Below the viewers, the Scene Detect graph displays the location of the video's cut points after the analysis. To the right, the cut list identifies the cuts and their timecodes.

6   In the lower-left corner of the window, click Auto Scene Detect.

As the analysis is run, the assumed edit points are marked with green lines in the Scene Detect graph and their timecodes are recorded in the cut list.

> **TIP** The height of the green cut lines indicates Resolve's level of confidence that a cut was correctly identified in that location. Cuts that fall under the magenta confidence line are omitted from the cut list and appear gray on the graph.
>
> If the video has many jump cuts and whip pans, the scene detection might place many cuts beneath this confidence line. To allow for less confident cuts to be included in the final cut list, drag down the magenta line until the edit lines turn green.

7   To review the edits, scrub through the timeline by dragging the orange playhead, or click inside the cut list, and press the Up and Down arrow keys to navigate and verify the cut points.

TIP You can also use keyboard shortcuts P (previous) and N (next) to jump between cut points.

A correctly identified cut will display a unique image in the left viewer, followed by two similar images in the next two viewers.

8 Navigate through the edits in the cut list until you reach scene 12.

Although Resolve detected a cut here, this is actually part of the same take. The false detection happened due to a headlight-caused lens flare that created enough of a visual change in the frame to be identified as the start of a new shot.

9 With the cut already selected, click Delete at the lower-left of the scene cut detection window to remove it.

TIP You can also press the + (plus) and minus - (minus) keys on your keyboard to Add and Delete cuts.

10 Continue pressing the Down arrow key to navigate through the cut list and ensure that all cuts are correctly located.

Toward the end of the timeline, you will find a large cluster of cut points. Dissolves and transitions are prone to misidentification and may show up as a series of rapid cuts.

11 Drag the playhead in front of this cluster, and press I to create an in point in the Scene Detect graph.

TIP Drag the scroll bar under the scene cut graph to zoom in on the cut points, if necessary.

12 Drag the playhead after the cut cluster, and press O to place an out point.

13 Under the right viewer, click the scissors icon to delete this batch of false cut points.

14 Press the Left and Right arrow keys to move through the video frame-by-frame to identify the exact cut point between the last clip and the solid white color matte at the end.

15 Click Add to add the edit to the cut list. A green line appears under your playhead to indicate an edit point. A new item also appears on the cut list with the frame and start timecode of the cut.

16 Ensure that no other cut points from the transition area have remained. If some have, drag the mouse over them and press Delete.

You have now addressed all the issues on this timeline. At this point, you should have 26 scenes in your cut list.

17 In the lower-right corner, click Add Cuts to Media pool.

TIP When working on longer films, or edits featuring jump cuts, reviewing scene cut detection can become a time-consuming process. You may choose to break up the work into several sessions, saving your progress as you go. You can save a scene cut in progress by accessing the options menu in the upper-right of the window and choosing Save Scene Cut. In the same option menu, you can also open a previously saved scene cut file.

18 If a dialogue box appears to inform you that your Project settings don't match the clips' frame rates and video formats, click Change to adjust the project timeline to accommodate your media.

19 Close the scene cut detection interface.

The commercial will now appear in your Media pool as a series of clips in the Video bin.

Before you can start grading your cut media, you will first place it in a timeline. To ensure that the clips fill the timeline in the correct order, you will organize your Media pool by clip timecode.

20 Switch to list view by click the list view button on the upper-right of the Media pool.

21 Click the Start TC column title to sort the clips by start timecode.

File Name	Reel Name	Start TC ∧	End TC	Duration	Frames	Type	Resolution
☐ Project 3 - The Long Work Day SCD.mov		01:00:00:00	01:00:05:00	00:00:05:00	120	Video	1920x1080
☐ Project 3 - The Long Work Day SCD.mov		01:00:05:00	01:00:09:01	00:00:04:01	97	Video	1920x1080
☐ Project 3 - The Long Work Day SCD.mov		01:00:09:01	01:00:13:07	00:00:04:06	102	Video	1920x1080
☐ Project 3 - The Long Work Day SCD.mov		01:00:13:07	01:00:17:08	00:00:04:01	97	Video	1920x1080

The clips are now ready to be placed into a timeline.

22 Enter the Edit page.

23 Select all the media in the Video bin by pressing Cmd-A (macOS) or Ctrl-A (Windows).

24 Right-click any of the selected clips, and choose Create New Timeline Using Selected Clips.

25 Name the new timeline **Project 03 - The Long Work Day Timeline**, and click Create.

A new timeline appears on the Edit page populated with the 28 selected clips in the Media pool.

26 In the Media pool, create a Timelines bin and place the timeline into it.

TIP Another workflow for importing self-contained video files using the scene cut detection tool is to not directly import the created subclips, but to save the EDL file of the scene cut results (using the option menu in the upper-right). Then import the EDL into the Media pool by right-clicking and choosing Timelines> Import > Pre-conformed EDL. This method will also produce a timeline full of cuts but will retain their trim points. This technique allows you to apply dissolves between the clips as needed.

You would ordinarily use this method of flattened video migration when working with remote clients that do not have access to servers or fast internet connections. Additionally, this workflow is often necessary when working on older projects in which the original media is no longer available and only the master export file remains. In both cases, it is crucial to use the highest-quality codec and file format possible, and avoid overlaid text, effects, or transitions that cannot be disabled in the flattened video file.

Understanding Timeline Resolutions and Sizing Palette Modes

In the next set of exercises, you will address the variety of ways in which you can impact the frame of your project in DaVinci Resolve. Specifically, you will learn how to change the resolution of your project, reframe individual shots, and sample portions of an image on a node level.

Switching Timeline Resolutions

With the **Project 03 - The Long Work Day** Timeline set up, you can now observe how changing its resolution will impact the image quality and secondary grading of a clip. First, you will need to set up the color spaces of the Project 03 - The Long Work Day Commercial project.

1   Open the Project settings, and navigate to the Color Management tab.

2   Set the Color Science to DaVinci YRGB Color Managed.

3   Set the Input Color Space for this footage as Blackmagic Design 4.6K Film.

4   Set the Timeline and Output Spaces to Rec.709 Gamma 2.4.

NOTE If the clips on the timeline do not change when color management is enabled, verify that they are not bypassing the Project settings. Select all the clips on the timeline, right-click any of the selected clips, and choose Input Color space > Project - Blackmagic Design 4.6K Film.

5   In the Color page, apply blue flags to clips 1, 5, and 15. You will be focusing on these clips in this lesson.

6   Use the Clips filter to display only the blue-flagged clips.

7   In the blue-filtered timeline, select clip 02.

8   Create a new node called **Vignette**.

9   Apply the Vignette preset to the window, and reposition and resize it to focus on the man at the window.

10   Drag the Offset wheel toward cyan to give the room a cool look. Drag the Gamma master wheel to the left to darken the edges of the frame.

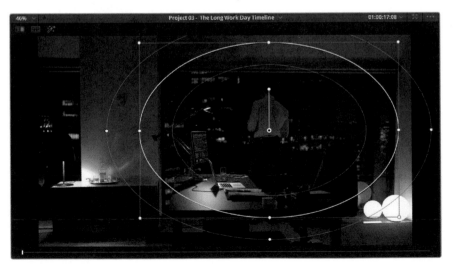

11 Open the Project settings, and enter the Master settings tab.

Project Settings: Project 03 - The Long Work Day Commercial

	Timeline Format
Presets	
Master Settings	Timeline resolution 1920 x 1080 HD
Image Scaling	For 1920 x 1080 processing
Color Management	Pixel aspect ratio ● Square
General Options	16:9 anamorphic
Camera RAW	4:3 standard definition
Capture and Playback	Cinemascope
	Timeline frame rate 24 frames per second
	Use drop frame timecode
	Playback frame rate 24 frames per second
	Enable video field processing

12 Change the Timeline Resolution to 3840 x 2160 Ultra HD, which is a 1.77:1 aspect ratio 4K resolution.

> **TIP** When rescaling media to a higher resolution (for example, converting 720p content to a 1080p timeline, or 1080p to a 4K timeline), you can activate a high-quality upscaling feature called Super Scale. To do so, in the Edit page, right-click a low-resolution clip, and choose Clip attributes. In the Video tab, in the Super Scale pop-up menu, choose 2x (or higher) to double the resolution. Doing so will substantially improve the method by which the image is upscaled in higher-resolution projects. However, this is a processor-intensive operation that may interfere with real-time playback.

13 Click Save to exit the Project settings.

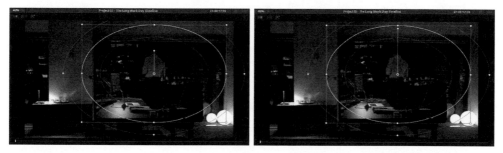

1920 x 1080   3840 x 2160

Compare the difference between the two resolutions. Note that the clip framing and positioning in the viewer has not changed at all. Additionally, the Power Window is rescaled to the new resolution while maintaining the placement in relation to the media clip.

This behavior is one of the most invaluable features of Resolve. The program is resolution independent, which allows you to change the frame size and aspect ratio of a project without affecting the positions of the clips, images, secondary grades, and generators created on the Edit or Color pages.

14   Reset the grade in clip 02.

4K to 1080p to 4K Workflow

Switching the Timeline resolution is an effective method for optimizing workstation performance during your editing stage. Doing so can ensure that clips are rendered and played in real time without lag. A common workflow for 4K footage is to set the timeline to 1920 x 1080 during the editing process, and set the Output Scaling (in the Master settings or the Deliver page) to 4K to restore the full resolution when rendering.

The proxy mode will continue to affect your image regardless of resolution. So, if you are reducing your timeline resolution for faster playback during editing or preliminary grading, consider turning off the Proxy Mode in the Playback menu to prevent further reduction of the image quality.

Also, be aware that the grading potential, as well as the accuracy, of key-dependent secondary grading tools such as the qualifier, is reduced at a lower image resolution. Therefore, you are advised to change the timeline to the full media resolution before grading.

Under the Timeline resolution presets of the Project settings, you also have the option of entering a custom resolution which will result in a non-standard video resolution at the aspect ratio of your choosing. Be aware that this method of changing the aspect ratio can be problematic in some projectors or video players. When outputting to equipment that recognizes standard video formats, it is a safer option to stick to a common (preset) resolution and apply blanking to change the aspect ratio.

TIP   Apply blanking to your timeline by clicking Timeline > Output Blanking, and choosing an aspect ratio. This method will preserve the original resolution of the video while permitting you to change the project aspect ratio.

Reframing Individual Clips

The Sizing palette becomes an increasingly versatile tool when you take advantage of its sizing modes. These modes allow you to switch the sizing focus from clips, to entire timelines, to individual nodes. In this exercise, you will rescale and reposition clips on an individual and timeline basis.

1   Enter the Project settings, and set the Timeline resolution to 1920 x 1080 HD.

2   In the blue-flag filtered timeline, click clip 03.

3   Enter the Sizing palette, and enter the Zoom value as **1.500** to scale up the image.

4   Click back to clip 02.

    Notice that clip 02 was not affected by the reframing of clip 03. In fact, every clip in the timeline, with the exception of clip 03, has remained unchanged because clip 03 was changed at the clip level (Input Sizing) in the Sizing palette.

5   Return to clip 03, and reset the Sizing palette.

6   It is necessary to remove filters when applying changes that affect the whole timeline. Use the Clips filter to display All Clips.

7   In the upper-right of the Sizing palette, in the pop-up menu, choose Output Sizing.

8   Enter the Zoom as **1.500** again.

9   Click the other clips in the timeline to verify that they have been altered by the change in scale.

    Sometimes, rescaling makes sense on a timeline-wide basis, such as when appropriating media to a different resolution or aspect ratio. However, reframing tends to be much more specific to the visual content of each shot.

10 Use the Clips filter to display only the blue-flagged clips.

    Let's reframe shots 02 and 03 based on content.

11 Change the Sizing palette mode back to Input Sizing.

12 In clip 03, change the Pan to **45.00**, and the Tilt to **50.00**.

13 In clip 02, change the Pan to **90.00**, and the Tilt to **-25.00**.

14 Switch between the clips to check that they have retained their Output Sizing zoom, but have adopted different pan and tilt values.

> **NOTE** This technique is often used in HD projects incorporating 4K footage, which can be zoomed up to 200% (on a 1080p timeline) before visual quality is degraded.

These changes used two modes (Input and Output) of the Sizing palette. Previously, you rescaled and reframed a wiped still using the Reference Sizing mode.

The full list of sizing modes and their impact on the image is as follows:

- **Edit sizing** reflects the transform changes applied to a clip in the Inspector of the Edit page.

- **Input sizing** reflects the sizing changes made to a clip in the Color page. It targets clips on the same level as Edit Sizing, but isolates the function to the Color page.

- **Output sizing** applies to the entire timeline.

- **Node sizing** applies to the selected node in the Node editor.

- **Reference sizing** applies to the reference movie or still that is visible in the viewer's wipe mode.

Sampling Visual Data with Node Sizing

Having the ability to change an image's sizing data at the node level permits some interesting creative and practical application. You could clone an image to display multiple versions of it within the viewer, or perform repair work by sampling portions of the image to be used for cover-up work.

In the following exercise, you will use node sizing to produce a creative layered look.

1 Reset the Input and Output sizing data from the previous exercise.

2 In the blue-flag filtered timeline, click clip 03.

3 Label node 01 as **Base**.

4 Create a new serial node called **Backplate**.

5   Press Option-L (macOS) or Alt-L (Windows) to create a Layer mixer node.

6   Rename the new node (node 04) which is connected to the Layer mixer as **Crop** and select it.

7   Open the Window palette.

8   Activate a linear window, and reposition the corners to capture the front half of the car.

9   Change all the Softness values to 0.00 to give the window a sharp edge.

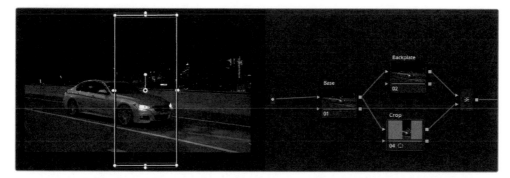

10 Open the Sizing palette, and set it to Node Sizing mode. From now on, all changes to the Sizing palette will only affect node 04 Crop.

11 Change the Zoom to 2.0 to scale up the linear window and its contents.

    Note that the backplate remains unchanged.

12 Pan the window (375.000) until you can no longer see the backplate to the right of the viewer.

13 Tilt the window upward (300.000) to see more of the road in the scaled-up node.

14 Select the Backplate node.

15 In the Sizing palette, pan the image left (-300.000) to place the car in the left-half of the viewer.

16 Reselect the Crop node to begin grading the car close-up.

17 Drag the Offset wheel toward blue to give the shot a cool metallic look.

18 Drag the Lift wheel toward red to slightly offset the blue in the shadows.

19 Increase the contrast and adjust the pivot of the image until it is significantly lighter than the original, but still contains pitch-black shadows and metallic highlights. Adjust the Offset master wheel, if necessary.

20 Play the clip to see the two versions of the footage simultaneously.

In layer-based compositing systems, this effect would only be possible by creating a second video track, duplicating the clip over itself, and using a crop tool. Due to its less efficient method of reusing video data, layer-based compositing tends to be more processor-intensive. Nodes provide a much cleaner approach to the duplication and resampling of RGB signals.

Creating Cover-ups with Patch Replacer ResolveFX

You can also use node sizing for more practical compositing solutions, such as sampling a portion of the video to cover up an undesirable artifact. This type of painting or cover-up work is often used to fix continuity errors or improve set design.

In this exercise, you will use the advanced Patch Replace ResolveFX to quickly perform cover-up work and automatically adjust the grade of the sampled area to match the destination.

> **NOTE** DaVinci Resolve Studio is required to complete the following exercise.

1   In the blue-flag filtered timeline, click clip 02.

This is a visually interesting shot with good set design and a great choice of location. However, one minor element is distracting from the luxurious office: the wall thermostat. Your aim is to remove the thermostat by covering it with a sample of a portion of the wall.

2   Label node 01 as **Coverup**.

3   Open the Open FX panel.

4   Find the ResolveFX Revival category, and drag the Patch Replacer effect onto the Coverup node.

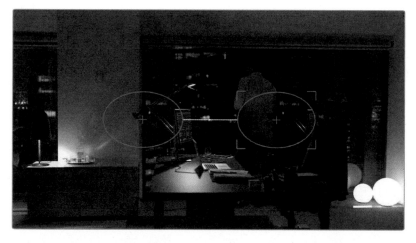

Two oval outlines appear in the viewer. The left oval represents the source patch, which is actively sampling the portion of the video under it. The right oval with the four corners is the target patch, and it is receiving visual data from the source and actively grading it to match its surroundings.

5   Drag the target patch over the wall, and resize it to outline the thermostat and its shadow.

6   Drag the source patch over an empty area of the wall near the target.

7   If necessary, zoom in on the viewer to refine the placements.

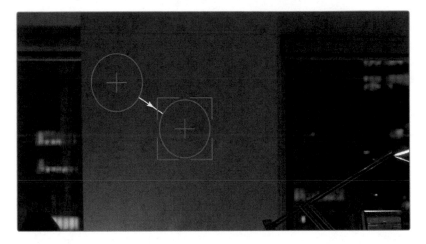

> **TIP** To navigate inside the viewer after zooming in, hold down your middle
> mouse button and drag in the viewer. If your scroll wheel does not have a click
> option, you can Shift-Option-drag (macOS) or Shift-Alt-drag (Windows) to move
> horizontally and vertically within the viewer.

The cover-up is successful, but only on the first frame of the clip. As soon as you play
back the video, the thermostat is revealed from behind the cover-up node. To complete
the composite, you will need to track the effect to the camera movement.

8   Press Shift-Z to fit the video frame to the viewer panel.

9   Open the Tracker palette, and in the upper-right pop-up menu, change its mode to FX.

To perform motion tracking, you will need to first specify a tracking point. Ideally,
you will want to identify the element you are covering up, or a trackable area that is
on the same plane as that element. In the case of this clip, the original thermostat is
an ideal tracking point.

10   Click the Coverup node name to bypass that node, and reveal the thermostat under
the patches.

11   In the lower-left corner of the Tracker palette, click the add tracker point button.

Blue crosshairs appear in the center of the frame. These crosshairs indicate the point of the image that will be analyzed for tracking.

12 Drag the crosshairs over the thermostat on the wall.

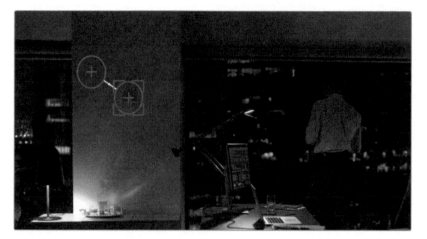

The crosshairs turn red when the default position is altered.

13 In the Tracker palette, click the track forward button to perform the track analysis.

14 After tracking is completed, click the Coverup node name to see the patches.

15 If necessary, in the lower-left corner of the viewer, turn off the on-screen controls to hide the patch and tracking point outlines.

16 Play the shot to check the accuracy of the cover-up. Make further adjustments to the size and placement of the source and target patches, if necessary.

The result is a clean cover-up of the wall that is ready for further editing and grading.

TIP You can perform this type of cover-up effect using Node Sizing. With a Backplate node in place, create a Layer node and use a Power Window to sample a clean portion of the video. In the Sizing palette, move the Layer node over the portion of the image you want to cover up. In the case of moving camera shots, begin the workflow by tracking the video with the standard window tracker before moving the Power Window over the sample area.

Node-based cover-ups are frequently employed to address the aesthetic needs of a scene, or to resolve issues that were not noticed during the shoot (for example, removal of visible set equipment, or covering spots on actors' faces). These workflows tend to work best on footage with little movement and good sample areas.

Using Keyframing

To understand keyframing, you need only to grasp the concept that you need just two keyframes to create any animation. And those keyframes need to communicate just two things to the program: their points in time and their values. By placing the keyframes at different points in the timeline, you indicate the length of time through which the change occurs, and by giving those keyframes individual values, you specify the nature of the change.

Animating Position Values with Dynamic Keyframes

Dynamic keyframes animate a gradual shift from one value to the next, which creates the effect of smooth change over time. In this exercise you will animate the transform values and the color grade of the shot to imitate a camera move and sunrise effect.

1   Select clip 01 on Project 03 - The Long Work Day Timeline.

The clip appears much darker and noisier than the rest of the footage on the timeline. This is because this shot was captured on a different camera than the rest of the media, and is being distorted by the color management.

2   Right-click clip 01, and choose Input Color space > Blackmagic Design 4K Film to correct the input color space.

The resulting image is a little flat. Before you can begin grading it creatively, you should expand its luminance range to fully take advantage of the colors and contrast.

3   Label node 01 as Balance.

4   Drag the Gain master wheel to the right (2.10) to increase the waveform spread and overall brightness of the image. Some noise issues are revealed in the low-light conditions. You will resolve these after the grade is completed.

The clip is a locked establishing shot. Even though it was captured in real-time, it has a time-lapse feel to it. In the next few exercises, you will introduce animation to the shot to imitate the fast passage of time in the environment.

Your first goal is to create a pan-and-zoom movement, starting from the wide shot and ending on the city skyline.

5   To the right of the palettes in the Color page, open the Keyframes editor.

The palette currently includes animation controls in two categories: the individual controls of node 01 (Corrector 1) and the Sizing value of the overall clip.

6   Create a new serial node and label it **Sunrise**. Corrector 2 appears in the list of the Keyframes palette.

Each new node you create will receive its own corrector category in the Keyframes editor.

7   To prepare to animate the motion in the image, expand the Sizing category.

8   Click the diamond-shaped keyframe symbol next to Input Sizing to activate animation in that palette.

9   While on the first frame of the clip, right-click the playhead in the Keyframes timeline, and choose Add Dynamic Keyframe.

The circular keyframe at the start of the clip become diamond-shaped.

10 Drag the playhead to the end of the clip duration in the Keyframes timeline.

11 With the Sizing palette in Input Sizing mode, change the Zoom to 1.500, the Pan to -400.000 and the Tilt to -200.000.

Two new dynamic keyframes are automatically added to the keyframes timeline. Additionally, two dimmed triangles indicate that a dynamic animation was generated.

12 Play back the clip to watch the animation in action. The shot begins with a wide view of the city and then quickly zooms in on the skyline in the distance.

> TIP If you click the Loop button in the viewer playback controls, the playhead will play the same clip over and over again instead of continuing through the timeline.

Changing Color Values Over Time with Dynamic Keyframes

Next, to animate the color values of the clip, you'll need to directly target the keyframe controls within the nodes.

1   In the blue flag-filtered timeline, drag the playhead back to the first frame of clip 01.

TIP You can click the expand button in the upper-right corner of the Keyframes editor to increase the interface size. Doing so will move all other palettes to the left of the Color page, giving you more room to focus on keyframing.

2 Select node 02, Sunrise.

   To imitate the look of the sun rising, you will first need to create a pre-dawn look.

3 Drag the Gamma master wheel to the left to darken the midtone ranges of the image, and then drag the Gamma Color Wheel toward blue to cool the temperature of the shot.

4 Accentuate the shadows and details in the skyline by increasing the Contrast in the adjustment controls.

5 Finally, reduce saturation to 30.00, to imitate the reduced perception of color in dark environments.

6 In the Keyframes palette, expand Corrector 2.

7 Click the keyframe symbol next to Color corrector to activate keyframing.

8 Right-click in the Keyframes timeline, and choose Add Dynamic Keyframe.

9 Drag the playhead to the last frame of the clip.

10 Grade the clip the way you want it to appear at the end of the animation.

    To imitate sunrise, drag the gain and offset master wheels right to brighten up the overall image.

11 Drag the Gamma and Gain Color wheel toward yellow and orange to warm up the image.

12 Return the saturation to 50.0 to more accurately represent the colors.

TIP   Press the [(left bracket) and] (right bracket) keys to navigate between keyframes in the Keyframes palette. This shortcut can save you time when comparing the different stages of an animation.

13   Play back the clip to see the colors animate over time.

Color temperature fluctuation is a very common reason to perform keyframed color grading. Shoots in which the camera operator frequently maneuvers from indoor to outdoor locations (documentaries, wedding videography, and so on) benefit greatly from these types of animated grade workflows.

Applying Dynamic Attributes

Though the animation in this example was successful, the zoom still appears a little artificial due to the linear nature of the animation. In the next exercise, you will simulate a more realistic camera zoom by altering the animation speed and style using dynamic attributes.

1   With clip 01 still selected, select and right-click the first keyframe in the Input Sizing property.

2   Choose Change Dynamic Attributes.

The dynamic attributes pop-up interface controls the behavior of the animation from the currently selected frame to the next frame.

3   Set the Start Dissolve value to 2. The almost-horizontal shape of the line at the start indicates that change will be very slow and gradual, before it accelerates and finishes in a linear fashion.

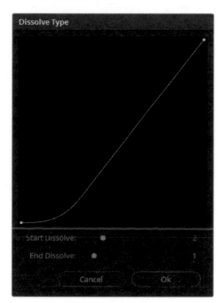

4   Click OK to confirm the change.

5   Play back the clip and note the slow start to the animation. This move makes the simulated zooming effect more realistic.

Using Static Keyframes

When creating a new keyframe in the editor, the alternative to dynamic is static keyframes. Static keyframes do not calculate change between values. Instead, they abruptly change the value of the clip like a switch.

You can combine static and dynamic keyframes within a single animation, such as when a change needs to be gradual, but to abruptly appear/disappear at the start or end of the animation--for example, with a lightbulb, that lights up abruptly and then gradually increases in brightness and temperature.

Mastering keyframe animation can take some getting used to, but in time, and with consistent practice, generating keyframes and creating changes can become a common and frequently utilized part of your grading workflow.

Applying Noise Reduction

Resolve's noise reduction feature runs on a powerful engine that is able to distinguish noise apart from environmental sounds by performing a temporal analysis of the video frames. This technique allows for a strong reduction of noise, while preserving a high level of detail in the subjects of the image. Applying the additional spatial method of noise reduction can further clean up the image by reducing overall noise patterns.

> **NOTE** DaVinci Resolve Studio is required to complete the following exercise.

1   In the blue flag-filtered Project 03 - The Long Work Day Timeline, click clip 01.

2   Drag the playhead to the last frame of the clip to see it at its brightest.

Due to the low light conditions in which this footage was captured, the brightening of the gamma and gain has revealed digital noise in the shadows and midtones.

3   For a better view of the noise detail in the image, change the viewer Zoom to 200%.

4   Create a new serial node after the Balance node (node 03) and label it **Denoise**.

5   Open the Motion effects palette.

This palette is divided into three control areas:

- **Temporal NR** analyses the video across several frames to isolate noise from detail. It tracks the motion of objects in the frame and excludes them from noise reduction processing to prevent unwanted artefacts.

- **Spatial NR** softens high-frequency noise while retaining the data in levels of high detail. This tool is extremely effective for reducing fine-grain noise that the Temporal NR missed.

- **Motion Blur** is not a noise-reduction tool, but uses the same analytical engine to produce its results. This tool helps make action shots more dynamic by allowing you to add motion blur to moving subjects.

6   Under Temporal NR, you will first need to choose the number of frames that will be averaged to separate the detail from noise. For this shot, which features no camera movement or moving subjects, an analysis of 2 is sufficient.

The higher the number, the more accurate the analysis will be, at the expense of extra processing time. However, a higher analysis rate could also produce artefacts in shots with overlapping moving subjects.

The Mo. Est. Type (Motion Estimation Type) setting enables you to indicate the method used to detect motion in the image. A setting of Faster prioritizes speed of output over quality, whereas Better will produce a finer result at the expense of extra processing time. Choosing None will bypass the motion detection feature and apply noise reduction to the entire image.

7   For clip 01, choose Better.

Motion Range allows you to indicate the speed at which the subjects are moving to exclude areas with motion blur from the noise reduction effect.

8   Clip 01 has almost no motion, so Small is a good choice.

The Temporal Threshold controls how aggressively noise reduction is applied to luma and chroma levels. By default, these options are linked; but if the image has monochromatic noise, it is advisable to unlink the two parameters and target the luma directly.

This is the setting that will activate noise reduction in the image, so you can begin with any number and then drag left or right to increase or decrease the effect.

9   Enter 5.0 as the starting Threshold.

To see how much the Temporal NR is affecting the image, you can use the Highlight tool to assess the pixel difference.

10 In the viewer, enable Highlight mode.

11 In the upper-right of the viewer, click the A/B icon to activate the Difference mode.

The patterns you see in the viewer show the amount of noise that has been removed from the original image.

12 Drag the Thresholds to the right to increase the severity of the noise reduction.

Good noise reduction   Noise reduction too aggressive

13 Stop adjusting when you start to recognize the outlines of objects on the horizon, which indicates that the noise reduction has become so aggressive that it is now removing legitimate visual information. Drag the Threshold left (10.0) until only noise remains.

The Motion value acts as a pivot for the point in which moving objects are excluded from noise reduction on the motion controls at the top of the panel. A lower value excludes larger areas of the image, whereas higher numbers assume less motion and target more of the image.

Because very little motion occurs in the image, a high Motion value of 60.0 is appropriate.

The Blend value allows you to blend the original image into the noise-reduced version. This adjustment can be helpful when the noise reduction is too aggressive, and areas of the image take on a plastic appearance.

14 Leave Blend unchanged for this clip.

15 Disable the Highlight view, and toggle the Grade Bypass to compare the image before and after the Temporal NR.

The noise reduction is substantial. However, there is still room for improvement by reducing the more generic noise patterns in the image.

> NOTE Because Temporal NR is designed to carefully avoid applying noise reduction to moving elements in a shot, it is best applied to locked-off images. In a shot with a quick pan or handheld camera motion, every element will be moving, which defeats the purpose of the Temporal NR analysis.

16 Under Spatial NR, set the reduction Mode to Enhanced.

As with Motion Estimation Type in the previous section, this setting is responsible for determining the speed/quality of the final output; though, in this case, Faster, Better and Enhanced refer to different analysis algorithms. Choosing Enhanced will produce a substantially improved output.

The Radius value indicates the area of the image that is analyzed to determine the noise type within the frame. The larger the area, the more accurate the analysis will be at the expense of processing speed.

17 For more subtle noise types, as in this image, a Radius setting of Medium is enough for a successful analysis.

As with the Temporal NR, the Luma and Chroma Threshold setting determines the intensity of the Spatial NR.

18 Change the Luma and Chrome Threshold to 40.0 to see a further reduction in the remaining image noise. As you did previously, use the Highlight tool to ensure that the details in the image are not too strongly affected.

Before noise reduction   After noise reduction

19 Press Cmd-D (macOS) or Ctrl-D (Windows) to bypass the Denoise node and compare the image before and after noise reduction. Pay particular attention to the preservation of the fine detail in the image—the Ferris wheel spokes and the windows in the buildings of the skyline.

Before moving on, it would be worth to check if changing the location of the Denoise node could improve the noise reduction of the image.

20 Select the Denoise node and press E to extract it from the pipeline.

21 Drag the Denoise node to the link between the RGB input and node 01 (Balance). This will perform noise reduction on the original RGB signal before any grading or animation takes place.

In this instance, the change softens the impact of the noise reduction and gives a better visual output.

22 Bypass the Denoise node before moving to the next exercise.

It is always advisable to use a dedicated node for noise reduction. After the noise is reduced to a satisfactory level, you can disable the denoise node before proceeding with the rest of the grading process. Deactivating the noise reduction node will reduce the amount of processing and caching the software will need to perform for playback.

Where should you place the noise reduction node?

Applying NR at the start of the node tree is advisable because it analyses and uses the original RGB data to reduce noise. However, this placement may potentially impact the precision of key-based selection methods (HSL curves, qualifier). Applying noise reduction at the end of the node tree can avoid this issue (if it is present), but can also produce a slightly less detailed image. When unsure, change the position of the NR node in the Node editor until you find the optimal position.

Optimizing Performance with Render Cache

Almost anyone who has done graphic-intensive work on a computer will be familiar with the frustration of experiencing lag when the workstation is incapable of processing the data in real time.

DaVinci Resolve offers a variety of methods for improving workstation performance. For example, by using Optimized Media, or any transcoded media workflows you can change the size and quality of the footage to ensure faster playback during editing.

Another powerful method for increasing playback speed is allowing Resolve to render your footage while the application is otherwise inactive. You can then play the cached media without the need to actively render effect-heavy clips.

Understanding Source and Sequence Caching

The process of rendering footage in the background, or generating a cache, in Resolve can be enabled on a variety of levels. In the following set of exercises, you will enable smart caching in your project and observe two early caching levels: source and sequence.

1   Enter the Edit page.

2   Choose Playback > Render Cache > Smart.

By using the Smart cache option, you are leaving it up to the software to choose which media or nodes are computationally intensive and require caching.

The first level at which caching takes place is the source. When using smart cache, it is generated for processor-intensive video formats such as H.264 and RAW. Because Project 03 - The Long Work Day Timeline is using media in an intermediary codec, which is already optimized for editing, the program is able to play it back in real time without performing source caching.

After the source cache, a sequence cache is generated in the Edit page when additional effects such as transitions, titles or generators are applied to clips in the timeline.

3   In the Edit page, open the Effects Library palette.

4   In the Titles folder under Toolbox, locate the Text title generator.

5   Drag the title generator onto video track 2, and extend its length to cover the first five clips of the timeline.

6   In the upper-right of the Edit page, open the Inspector palette.

7   Click inside the text box under the Rich Text heading, and enter the project name The Long Work Day.

   A red line appears over the timeline to indicate that a cache is being generated for all the media under the title tool.

When the rendering process is complete, the line turns blue.

Generating Node Cache

The node cache appears in the Node editor of the Color page after the application of grades and effects. Like the source cache, when smart cache is enabled, rendering will occur only when Resolves deems the processes to be intensive.

1   Enter the Color page.

2   Change the timeline filter to show All Clips.

3   At the top of the page, click the Timeline button to view the timeline ruler in the Color page and see your video tracks and cache processes.

4   Note that the sequence cache over the title generator is still active. Because you do not need to see or cache the titles during your grading work, you can disable them by clicking V2 on the timeline ruler.

5   Click clip 01.

6   The Denoise node was bypassed in a previous exercise. Click the Denoise node name to activate it.

The timecode above the clip thumbnail will turn red to indicate that it is in the process of caching. Additionally, the node name and number will turn red in the Node editor for the same reason.

The cache line on the timeline ruler will eventually turn blue as caching is completed.

7   Create a serial node after the Sunrise node, and label it BW (node 04).

8   In the adjustment controls, drag the Sat value to 0.

Your image retains its sunrise animation, though now it is displayed in only black and white. The BW node did not turn red and will not require caching because the standard color-grading controls are usually not intensive enough to disrupt the playback of the clip.

Adding the BW node has also not enacted a re-cache of the Denoise node because the denoising is not affected by the changes made in the BW node. If you follow the path of the RGB signal, it is denoised before it is desaturated, and so the same denoised version of the cache can continue to be used.

9   Click the Denoise node, and press E to extract it.

10   Drag the node over the connector at the end of the pipeline to place it after the BW node.

The Denoise node turns red as it re-caches the new RGB signal.

11   After the Denoise node turns blue, click the BW node, and adjust the Contrast in either direction.

This time, the change prompts the Denoise node to turn red and require a new cache. The BW change affected the RGB input of the Denoise node, which has to perform a new render using the new RGB signal.

Utilizing Smart Cache and User Cache Modes

As you have seen, the decision to render the clips on every level of the workflow is made within the background processes of the software. Smart cache allows you to continue to focus on your project while Resolve detects when rendering is necessary to enable faster playback.

However, at times, you might want to entirely take over the decision of which clips need to be rendered. For that, you can enable user cache, which will not perform any rendering on your media until you directly tell it to.

1   Choose Playback > Render Cache > User.

The blue highlights on clip 01 and the Denoise node will disappear when automated caching is disabled. From now on, all caching will occur only on your command.

This is a mode that some colorists prefer to work in when they do not wish background caching to occur throughout the project. A reason might be because they are using RAW media and want to cache only the clips that they are actively working on, instead of the entire timeline.

2   Click clip 01.

3   Right-click the Denoise node, and choose Node Cache > On. The node name turns blue once again and caching is performed.

When working on a larger project, you could potentially use the Clips filter to isolate clips with noise reduction, and manually cache them to avoid enabling smart cache.

In addition to selecting individual nodes in user cache mode, you can manually render the entire node tree of a clip.

4   Right-click clip 05, and choose Render Cache Color Output.

The clip's timecode will turn red in the timeline while the nodes remain white. In this scenario, the entire node pipeline is cached, which results in even faster playback when compared to rendering individual nodes. However, it also means that making changes to any of the nodes in the pipeline will require that the clip be re-cached.

5   In the clip 05 Node editor, add a new serial node called Magenta Look.

6   Drag the Offset Color Wheel toward magenta to add color to the clip.

Although the process of adding color to the clip is not processor intensive, the clip immediately turns red in the timeline because a new cache is generated for the entire pipeline.

Configuring Cache Quality

When you play media in the viewers of the Edit and Color pages, you can see the current frame rate in the GPU status indicator, in the upper-left of the viewer.

A green light indicates that the media is being played in real time. A red light indicates lag, with the numerical value displaying the actual frame rate. Caching should result in the GPU status indicator outputting a green light during playback. If it does not, you should consider lowering the proxy mode resolution, or reducing the quality of the cache enable for faster review.

1   Open Project settings, and click the Master settings tab.

2   Scroll down until you see the Optimized Media and Render Cache section.

The Render cache format field allows you to set up the quality and format of your cache data.

Lowering the cache quality will reduce your cache file size, and prevent your hard drive from filling up too quickly with cached data. However, this will occur at the expense of the visual quality of the cache in your viewer. Avoid reducing cache quality if precision of color, luminance, and key data is important.

Inversely, raising the cache quality will ensure a faithful reproduction of your image data, at the expense of producing very large rendered files.

3   Set the Render cache format to one of the full quantization formats (444 or 4444) in preparation for the upcoming lessons.

Beneath the Render cache format menu are a few checkbox options.

You can specify the amount of time that needs to pass before background caching begins in smart cache mode. By default, it is five seconds, but you can extend it if you prefer to tweak your settings at a leisurely pace when grading.

Additionally, you can enable automated transition and composite rendering when in user mode, which will mimic the behavior of smart cache mode.

4   Select "Automatically cache transitions in User Mode".

5   Press Save to exit the Project settings.

Clearing a Cache

Wherever clips are cached (in the Edit page, Color page, or on individual nodes), a copy of the visual cache data is stored on your disc drive. Eventually, it might be necessary to remove this data to make room for more caching, or to delete unnecessary materials from older projects.

1   Choose Playback > Delete Render Cache > Unused.

A prompt will ask you to confirm if you would like to delete the unused cache.

2   Choose Yes. The media in the timeline remains rendered, while all previous cache versions of the clips are removed.

Other options for deleting the render cache allow you to delete all cached media, or selected clips on the timeline. It is important to remember that no actual media is affected by clearing a cache, and even if you accidentally delete the cache that is currently used in your project, it will be regenerated when it is next needed.

> **TIP** Occasionally, you might come across a graphic anomaly when the viewer in the Color page is outputting visual data that does not match the changes you made to a clip. For example, a Media Offline message appears when you are certain the media is connected. Clearing the render cache will remove the program's memory of the clip render and force it to re-render the clip correctly.

NOTE Cached media is placed in the folder specified in the Project settings under the Working Folders of the Master settings. By default, the Cache folder is located on the first Media storage location (Preferences > System) of your database; but to optimize playback, you may want to redirect it to a drive other than the one that contains the Resolve application and your project files.

Using proxies or offline media is vital for a clean editing workflow; but their use is discouraged for the grading process because they do not offer an accurate representation of the image when its colors are graded (or when qualifier selections are made). For this reason, the render cache is the recommended optimization method.

Self-guided Exercises

Complete the following exercises in the unfiltered Project 03 - The Long Work Day Timeline to test your understanding of the tools and workflows covered in this lesson.

Clip 02 - Use node sizing to cover up the speed limit signs at the top of the frame.

Clip 08 - Use dynamic and static keyframes together with the Highlights master wheel to flicker the lights in the garage.

Clip 15 - Generate a node before the base node and apply noise reduction.

When you've completed this exercise, you can open the Project 03 - The Long Work Day Commercial COMPLETED.drp and review the Lesson 7 Timeline to compare your work with a finalized version.

Lesson Review

1   Which function is used to automatically add cut points to a self-contained video file?

2   True or False? If you change the timeline resolution of a project, you will need to go over your secondary grade nodes and manually resize all the power windows to fit the new resolution.

3   Where can you animate the sizing and color properties of a clip?

4   What are dynamic keyframes?

5   True or False? Noise reduction should only be applied to node 01 of any clip.

Answers

1   Scene Cut Detection.

2   False. DaVinci Resolve is resolution independent, which means that all secondary tools will automatically resize themselves to fit the new resolution of the project.

3   Keyframes palette.

4   Keyframes that gradually change a value between two points in time.

5   False. Noise reduction can be applied to any node in the pipeline, based on necessity.

Using Groups in the Grading Workflow

In this lesson, you will focus on an organizational feature of the Color page that enables clip grouping based on shared visual criteria.

Although generating and organizing groups is incredibly simple, their usage opens up a new grading workflow within the Color page. In addition to applying group-wide grades via the Node editor, the grouping feature allows timeline filtering based on group name and the activation of a split screen to compare clips in the same group.

Time

This lesson takes approximately 45 minutes to complete.

Goals

Creating a Group

When incorporating groups into a grading workflow, your first task is to choose a grouping strategy for the timeline. Depending on the nature of a project, you can base groups on locations, scenes, color temperature, shot size, or the criteria of your choice.

In the commercial project in this lesson, you will create groups to differentiate between scenes based on locations and times of day.

1   Open the Project 03 - The Long Work Day Timeline.

2   Enter the Color page.

3   Click clip 06, and Shift-click clip 13 to select the eight consecutive garage clips in the timeline.

4   Right-click any of the highlighted clips, and choose Add to Current Group.

A green link symbol appears in the lower-right corner of the clips to indicate their group relationship.

5   Right-click any of the grouped clips, and choose Groups > Group 1 > Rename.

6   Enter the group name **Garage**. These clips will now be linked when you start utilizing the group-level Node editor in later exercises.

Upon closer inspection, it appears that clip 13, the highway shot, does not belong in this scene, and therefore, should not be included in this group.

7   Right-click clip 13, and choose Remove from Group.

You can also use Groups for filtering purposes.

8   In the timeline, hold the Cmd-click (macOS) or Ctrl-click (Windows) clips 02 and 13.

9   Right-click one of them, and choose Add into a New Group.

10   Enter the group name **Highway**.

The link symbols on the Garage group disappear, and are now visible only in the Highway group. Now, the green link symbols will appear only when a grouped clip is selected.

The two Highway clips are relatively far apart on the timeline, so matching them could be tedious if you have to constantly navigate up and down the timeline to compare them.

11   Select Clips > Grouped > Highway.

The two highway clips are now side-by-side and can be quickly assessed and matched while pressing the Up and Down arrow keys.

12   Select Clips > All Clips to remove the timeline filter.

You'll need to create one more group in preparation for the exercises in this lesson.

13   Scroll down the timeline, select clips 19 to 26, and add them to a new group called **Home**.

Adopting Groups in a Classic Color Grading Workflow

With your clips sorted into groups, you can now proceed to choose the modes in which their grading will be targeted--from individual adjustments to group-wide uniform changes. Doing so will allow a much faster and more precise workflow in which you'll no longer need to duplicate and reapply grades to each individual clip. By reducing this duplication of effort, you'll also have less chance of mistakes creeping into the workflow. Instead of readjusting specific nodes on multiple clips or keeping track of dozens of stills, you may tweak a group grade to amend all of a scene's clips at once.

The following figure shows how the classic color grading workflow, previously expressed as a node tree structure in Lesson 1, can be translated into group-based node structures.

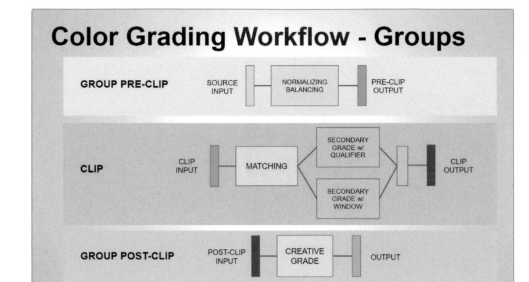

The following is a list of available grading modes in the Node editor and their relationships to the traditional grading workflow:

- **Group pre-clip** allows you to normalize footage with common luminance ranges and address obvious tint or temperature issues.
- **Clip** mode enables you to address the individual needs of each clip in the group, including matching and secondary grade adjustments.
- **Group post-clip** is best utilized for creative scene grading. By this stage, your clips are matched, and their individual secondary requirements have been met. Matching the clips ensures that the creative grade is uniformly applied, and requires only minimal tweaking on a clip-by-clip level.
- **Timeline** will affect every clip on the active timeline of your project. Color correction and creative grading is not recommended at this stage, but you could use this mode for artificial grain or applying vignettes and effects to short-form projects.

This breakdown suggests the order in which to address and process visual data, but you should not see it as a strict order of operations when grading. As with a standard grading workflow, it is entirely acceptable (and expected) to jump between group levels to make adjustments throughout the entire grading process.

Applying Base Grades at Pre-clip Group Level

With your groups identified and labelled, you can now establish a starting tonal range for your clip groups and address any obvious temperature and tint issues through the process of normalization.

It is important to keep in mind that all clips in the group are affected by changes, so avoid focusing too strongly on achieving a perfectly neutral appearance for any single shot. Instead, pick a key shot that is representative of most of the footage in the group and apply the necessary grades, or LUTs, that will give you a good starting point for matching at the next grading stage.

Adjusting Exposure in a Group

In this exercise, you will set up a tonal range and address some overshot highlights that are present in every clip in the group.

1   Set the Clips filter to display only the Garage group clips in the timeline.

2   Navigate among the clips in the timeline and analyze their waveforms.

There is some waveform variation among the clips which will require independent balancing and matching, but there are also some waveform consistencies.

First, the shadows on most of the clips are at a good starting position and will only need minor tweaking. And second, every clip has areas of over-exposure that you can address uniformly.

3   In the Garage group timeline, click clip 05.

This clip features a wide range of data that reflects the luminance ranges and environmental content of the other clips of the Garage group. This makes it a good choice as a key shot for the pre-clip grade.

4   In the pop-up menu at the top of the Node editor, switch to Group Pre-Clip mode. All the adjustments you are about to make will be applied to the whole group.

5   Label node 01 as Exposure.

6   In the custom curves, create a control point in the upper midtones of the YRGB-ganged master curve.

7   Drag the white point of the curve down to reduce the brightness in the highlights. Keep an eye on the waveform as you do so. Stop dragging the point before you start losing detail on the floor of the garage.

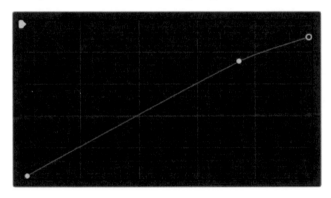

8   While still in the custom curves palette, raise the H.S. (high soft) value to about 90 to further bring down the overshot highlights, while retaining the finer differences in the upper luma ranges.

You will see a visible improvement to the over-exposed areas on the garage floor.

Before   After

9   Click clip 01 in the Garage group timeline.

10 Press Cmd-D (macOS) or Ctrl-D (Windows) to bypass the Exposure node and compare the clip's original luminance ranges to the adjustment you just made.

Before   After

You've created a better starting point for all the clips in the scene without significantly altering their overall ranges while still leaving yourself plenty of space and color quality to perform matching and creating grading down the line.

Using the Color Checker to Normalize a Group

Another method of normalizing the tonal range and balance in a sequence of clips is by referring to the calibration charts that were captured at the start of the scene shoot. Calibration charts allow for a type of automated balancing that gives you a much more accurate output than regular auto-balancing due to their reliable luminance ranges and meticulously designed color swatches.

1   Change the Clips timeline filter to display only the clips in the Home group.

These clips feature a color checker clip that you can use to quickly calibrate the group's Color space and gamma. A shot of the color checker is usually captured at the start of every new scene, light change, or location during filming to facilitate the quick normalization of clips in that sequence.

2   Ensure that the Node editor is still in group pre-clip mode.

3   In the Home group timeline, click clip 01.

4   Label node 01 as Color Match.

5   In the left palettes of the Color page, open the Color Match palette.

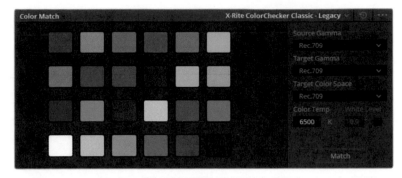

6   In the pop-up menu in the lower-left of the viewer, choose the Color Chart tool.

7   Drag the corners of the color chart interface to the corners of the color checker chart in the image. Ensure that the small squares in the middle of the color chart outline are filled with the colors they are meant to be analyzing. Any interference with the black chart borders, or the man's fingers, will affect the quality of this analysis.

8   At the top of the Color Match palette, verify that X-Rite ColorChecker Classic - Legacy is chosen. This selection is based on the version and type of color checker chart in use.

9   Set the Source Gamma to Gamma 2.4.

The RGB signal of the image is processed after its colors are remapped by the color management feature of the Project settings. Gamma 2.4 is the gamma level indicated as the output Color space in the color management of the project.

10   Change the Target Gamma to Gamma 2.4 to retain the same gamma range as the rest of your color-managed timeline while still balancing the colors of the sequence.

11   Click Match at the bottom of the Color Match palette. There will be a slight shift in color, most notably in the skin of the man, as the clip is balanced according to the chart.

The rest of the clips in the timeline have now adopted the automated color balance. However, because the sky is also significantly over-exposed in most of the shots, it makes sense to begin addressing this at the pre-clip level.

12   Create node 02 and label it Highlights.

13   Click clip 04.

This clip is a better candidate as a key shot because it features more of the environment than clip 01. It also has slightly less overexposure from the mid shots, which will prevent you from making the scene too dark prior to the matching process.

An alternative to using the curves palette when reducing over-exposure in a shot is to adjust the Highlights value.

14   In the Primaries wheels palette, open the second page of the Adjustment Controls, and lower the HL (Highlights) field to -80.

Before   After

Once again, the result is an image with a preliminary normalized grade that leaves the full gamma range and Color space available for the colorist to adjust in the upcoming grading stages.

TIP When working on a project that utilizes conversion LUTs, the pre-clip group level is the stage at which the LUTs are applied.

Making Clip-specific Adjustments at the Clip Group Level

By default, the standard Node editor applies grade changes on a clip-by-clip basis. It is the ideal way to match footage and make secondary amendments. When working with groups, you continue to have access to the Node editor in clip mode.

Matching Shots at the Clip Group Level

Before you can apply a creative grade to a group of clips, it is important to ensure that all of those clips match in terms of tint, temperature, and the distribution of luminance levels.

1   Filter the timeline to only show the Garage group clips.

2   Switch the Node editor to Clip mode.

3   Select clip 01. At first glance, the shot appears to be substantially brighter than the other clips in the scene.

4   Drag the viewer playhead to the end of clip 1.

When the man enters the garage, the shot appears to be exposed similarly to the others in the sequence and will not require aggressive balancing.

5 By default, thumbnail images in the timeline represent the first frame of a clip. Drag within the thumbnail of a clip to change the frame chosen for the thumbnail.

When comparing and balancing clips, remember that the first frame is not always the most reliable choice, and you should always play through the entire clip before making a grading decision. In this case, you can leave clip 01 as it is.

6 Select clip 04. This shot is definitely darker than the rest of the sequence.

7 Right-click clip 05, and choose Wipe Timeline Clip to enable the wipe mode in the viewer.

8 Open the Sizing palette in reference sizing mode, and pan clip 05 to more clearly see the man in the wide shot.

9   Press Option-F (macOS) or Alt-F (Windows) to expand the viewer and get a better view of the differences between the clips.

10 Open the Waveform scope (with active RGB channels) to view a graphic representation of the luminance differences between the clips. Just as in the viewer, the waveform is split along the wipe line.

11 Label node 01 in clip 04 as Match.

12 Drag the Gain master wheel up to brighten the midtones and highlights of the image. Keep an eye on matching the floor, walls and lights to the reference image.

13 Drag the Lift master wheel down slightly to create a matching balance with the midtones and shadows in the reference waveform.

14 Clip 04 has a significant green tint in its shadows. Drag the Lift wheel toward magenta until the tint in the man's suit is neutralized.

When the suit begins to match the one in the reference, the remainder of the room will start to look too magenta. A great tool to address this is the tint, which is designed to eliminate green/magenta casts made by fluorescent lighting.

15 In the adjustment controls, drag the tint setting to the left until the upper midtones match the ones in the reference image.

16 If a coolness remains in the image, drag the Gamma color wheel toward yellow to offset it.

The waveforms don't match. Are the clips really color matched?

When matching clips using waveforms, your goal is not always to make the waveforms look identical. Rather, it is to use the reference waveform as a guide to inform the overall spread of the luminance data, the heights of the brightest parts of the image, and the depths of the shadows.

In this example, clip 04 will always have a waveform that is concentrated at the bottom of the graph because it features a mid close-up of the man and his dark suit.

In clip 05, the suit occupies a very small part of the shot and appears in the waveform as a small dip to the shadows--the depths of which are now matched. Likewise, the lights in both waveforms follow a similar trajectory.

Lastly, the overall waveform in clip 04 has been spread out to a similar distance to clip 05. Bypass the grade in clip 04 to compare how compressed the waveform used to look.

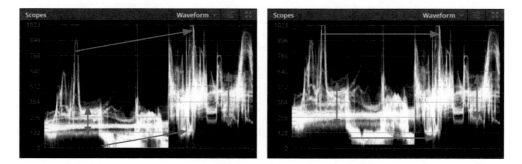

17 Press Option-F (macOS) or Alt-F (Windows) to exit the enhanced viewer mode, but leave the wipe mode on.

18 Click clip 07.

The clip colors are already a good match for the rest of the timeline, but the shot is too bright overall which will affect the quality of the post-clip grade.

19 Drag the Offset master wheel left to darken the shadows to the same level as the rest of the clips in the timeline.

20 Increase the contrast to expand the overall spread of the waveform trace. A good reference to watch as you adjust the image luminance is the garage ceiling, which should match in all shots.

21 Reset the Reference Sizing mode of the Sizing palette.

Making Secondary Adjustments at the Clip Level

Along with matching the clips of various groups, the clip level is where you would address secondary grading requirements. These ranges include making technical corrections to the shot (skin tone, fixing oversaturation/overexposure, node-based coverups, and so on), as well as creative amendments such as changing the hue of a specific element, and sky replacement.

In the following exercise you will address the overexposed appearance of the sky in the mid shots of the Home group in order to create a single cohesive look throughout the timeline.

1 Filter the timeline to show only the Home group clips.

2 Click clip 03. The sky in this mid shot is brighter than in the wide master shot.

3 Use clip 04 as a reference for the sky by choosing Wipe Timeline Clip in the contextual menu.

4 Right-click the viewer, and choose Invert Wipe to switch the positions of the clips in the viewer. Doing so will give you a better reference for the portion of the sky in clip 03 that you are trying to match.

5 Use the reference sizing transform controls to move the wide shot and get a better overview of the environment and the man in it.

6   In clip 03, label node 01 Sky Gain.

7   Open the Primaries bars in the Color wheel palette.

8   Drag the Gain Y bar down to reduce the brightness in the highlights of the image without affecting saturation.

9   Drag the Gamma Y bar up to undo the darkening of the midtones. Keep an eye on the man's shirt and trousers as a reference for the necessary brightness.

10 Drag the Lift Y bar down slightly to return the shadows to the same range as the rest of the clips in the sequence.

11 Increase contrast and adjust the pivot until the man's trousers are better matched to the reference image.

12 Press Cmd-W (macOS) or Ctrl-W (Windows) continuously to get a better overview of the sky in clip 03 as you match.

The sky's saturation and luminance in clip 03 changes from left to right because of the half-opened glass door, which is creating an ND filter effect to the left side. Be mindful that you are matching to the sky behind the glass door in clip 04.

With clip 03 matched, you can now copy its Sky Gain node to other mid shots from the same take.

13 Click clip 02. At first glance, it appears not to need the Sky Gain node.

14   Drag the playhead to the last frame of clip 02. As the camera pans, it reveals the window and the overexposed sky behind it.

15   Middle-click clip 03 to copy the Sky Gain node into clip 02.

Because this clip includes substantially darker areas at its start than the other clips, it is a good idea to use a secondary grade to isolate the node to affect just the sky as the camera pans to it.

16   Open the Window palette, and place a linear window around the sky in clip 02.

17   Open the Tracker palette, and analyze backward to get the linear window to follow the motion of the camera pan.

When the window remains in the shot after the sky leaves the frame, you can manually adjust the motion of the window by using the frame mode of the tracker.

> **NOTE** Revisit the "Tracking obscured objects" section of Lesson 3 for a reminder of how to use Frame mode to manually adjust windows.

18 Play back the clip to verify that the tracking looks natural.

Intermediary Matching Between Clips

At times, you will want to grade shots to show a gradual change in color or temperature between clips. It is not strictly a color match, but rather, an intermediary grade designed to transition between clips with different looks without jarring the viewer.

In this exercise, two clips captured at sunrise are intercut with media captured later in the day. You will match the daylight clip between them, and then grade the preceding clip to suggest a natural change in sunlight from the first half of the timeline to the second.

1   Cmd-click (macOS) or Ctrl-click (Windows) clips 04 to 07 to select them.

2   In the viewer, enable split screen.

3   In the pop-up menu in the upper-right of the viewer, choose Selected Clips.

4   Press Option-F (macOS) or Alt-F (Windows) to expand the viewer.

5   In the split-screen viewer, ensure that clip 06 (lower-left) is selected.

6   Label node 01 as Match.

7   Drag the Gain wheel toward yellow until the color of the sky matches the skies in the surrounding clips.

8   Reduce the contrast in the adjustment controls until the window frames and furniture shadows have the same low contrast as the surrounding sunrise clips.

9   To reduce the resulting orange cast in the room, open the Lum Vs Sat curve and reduce the saturation of the brightest parts of the image.

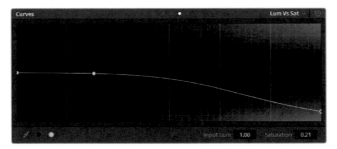

10 Finally, open the Log wheels and drag the Shadow Color Wheel toward blue to offset some of the brown in the black point of the image.

11 Copy the Match node grade of clip 06 into the first node of clip 04.

    To ensure a smooth transition between clips 03 and 05, you will want to reduce the severity of the grade in clip 04.

12 Open the Key palette, and change the Key output Gain to 0.500. The grade intensity is halved, and the original colors of the image now show through for a smooth transition between the first and second halves of the scene.

13 Press Option-F (macOS) or Alt-F (Windows) to exit the enhanced viewer mode.

14 Exit the split-screen viewer.

Creating a Unifying Look using the Post-Clip Group Level

When you achieve a color consistency in the clips within your groups, you are ready to move on to the final post-clip group level in which you will design and apply creative grades on a scene-by-scene basis. This is the stage at which other members of the creative process, such as the director and DP, would discuss the aesthetic needs of the shots and where you would create a series of test grades and LUTs.

Applying a Post-clip Grade with an External Reference

In this exercise, you will work with a reference image that a client has shared with you. You will import it into the gallery and treat it as a still for visual comparison.

1 Filter the timeline to show only the Garage group clips.

2 Switch the Node editor to group post-clip mode.

3 Click clip 07. This is the key shot you will use to grade the rest of the group.

4 To import an external reference image, right-click in the gallery, and choose Import.

5 In your file browser, navigate to the BMD 14 CC - Project 03 folder.

If you do not see any images in the folder, ensure that your browser window is specified to identify All Files as opposed to just the default .dpx format files.

6   Select the FK_Bridge_Reference.png image, and click Import.

7   Double-click the still to display it in the viewer.

Clients often use visual references from other films to communicate their desired looks for a project. In this case, the highly-stylized reference image points toward a scene with cool, dark shadows and vibrant midtones.

First, let's match the contrast and cold look of the reference shot.

8   Label node 01 as **Dark Blue**.

9   In the custom curves palette, drag the master curve black point across the bottom of the graph until the shadow under the car is almost pitch black.

10 Shape the master curve into an S-curve to add contrast to the midtones, while bringing some intensity into the lights within the image.

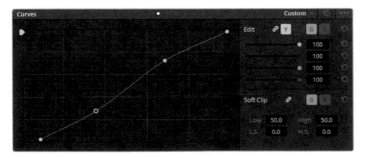

11 Drag the Offset wheel toward cyan to create a strong blue tone throughout the image.

12 Drag the Lift wheel toward red to undo some of the coolness in the shadows and make them slightly more neutral.

13 Drag the Gamma wheel toward magenta to reduce the green tint in the image and create a soft pink definition in the back of the garage compared to the blue foreground.

You can address the over-saturated blue headlight reflections on the floor in the Lum vs Sat curve of the Curves editor.

14 Click the white swatch under the curve graph and drag it down until the reflections are not oversaturated. Keep an eye on the other colors in the image to ensure you are not desaturating any prominent elements, like the columns or the hood of the car.

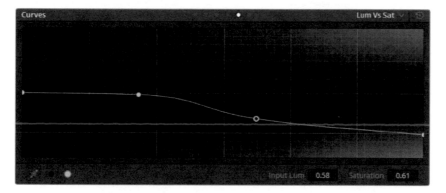

The overall temperature and tonal range of the scene is complete. You can now place a second node to enhance the garage's red columns and pipes.

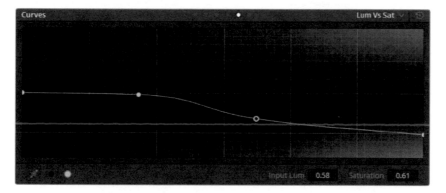

It's not common to create secondary grades in post-clip group Node graphs; but when the scenes have a consistent color scheme, it can work.

You will get a better secondary grade result if you use the original RGB signal of the clip instead of the RGB signal coming out of the heavily-graded and contrasted Dark Blue node.

15 Create a new Parallel Mixer node, and label it **Red Pipes**.

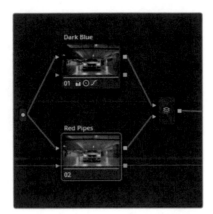

16 In the HSL curves, open the Hue vs Sat HSL curve.

17 Click the red swatch at the bottom of the palette, and increase the Sat by 50%. Doing so enhances the reds in the image, but also makes them a little distracting due to their unnatural brightness.

18 In the Hue vs Lum HSL curve, click the red swatch, and reduce the Lum by 50%. This darkens the red colors and matches them more closely to their environment.

> **TIP** To bypass the entire node tree within a specific level grade, press Option-D (macOS) or Alt-D (Windows). Doing so will leave your other node levels intact so you can assess the changes you have made within the current clip level.

Adjusting Clips after a Post-clip Grade

Occasionally, a post-clip grade will emphasize or reveal inconsistencies in the clips, which will result in mismatched grades. In such cases, you will need to return to clip mode in the Node editor to make further adjustments.

In this exercise, you will return to the clip mode to apply an effect to the key shot, and then fix a discrepancy that was revealed in one of the shots on the timeline.

1   With clip 07 still selected, return the Node editor to clip mode. You will be applying an effect to the final clip to make the highlights more dramatic.

2   Create a second node, and label it **Headlights**.

3   Open the Open FX panel.

4   Find the ResolveFX Light category, and drag the Aperture Diffraction effect onto the Headlights node.

The result is an optical effect that mimics the diffraction of light. The settings in the OpenFX panel allow you to refine the pattern, intensity, and color of the effect.

5   Under Aperture Controls, change the Iris Shape to Square.

> **TIP** In the Output category of the Aperture Diffraction settings, change Select Output to Diffraction Patterns Alone to get a clearer view of the light patterns as you adjust the settings. Change the output back to Final Composite to see the final result.

6   Under Compositing Controls, increase the Brightness to 0.600.

7   Increase the Colorize value to 0.300, and use the swatch underneath to change the Color to magenta.

This simple effect dramatizes the final shot of the sequence as the car drives away. A variety of light-based effects in the Open FX panel enable you to stylize your shots and make features "pop" in subtle or exaggerated ways.

Next, you will check the remainder of the garage sequence to ensure that all shots match.

8   Navigate through the clip timeline, and check the other clips for consistency.

You can see that the upper midtones in clip 06 are substantially bluer when compared to the environments in clips 05 and 07. Clip 06 is also fairly dark, which is making it difficult to see the actor's face.

9   Enable the Wipe Timeline contextual menu to compare clip 06 to clip 07.

10 Change the Node editor to clip mode.

11 Label node 01 as **Match**.

12 Drag the Offset wheel slightly toward orange to remove the blue dominance in clip 06, and in the adjustment controls, increase the contrast slightly.

13 In the custom curves, isolate the lower midtones of the Y curve, and drag the curve upward to brighten up the man's face.

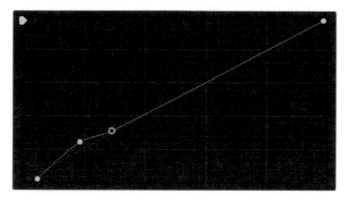

The overall blue dominance of the shot is reduced, and the man's face is more clearly visible.

The convenience of the group grading workflow is that no single stage or node is permanent. It is easy to jump between the different stages and tweak them as required, all while seeing the final output in the viewer.

Applying Timeline Level Grades

The timeline level is available in the Node editor whether you use a groups workflow or not. As the name implies, adjustments made at this level affect every timeline clip uniformly. This technique can sometimes be useful for image property applications such as modifying blanking, adding a vignette, or inserting grain. It is not as strongly advised for grading purposes, but can be applied to great effect in short video projects with consistent base colors.

In this exercise, you will apply a film grain look to the entire project, followed by the data burn-in details that will make it easier to keep track of timecodes and clip names during the feedback stage of post-production.

Apply Film Grain to an Entire Timeline

Artificial film grain is sometimes added to digital media for a variety of reasons. Occasionally, film grain is required to make the film look outdated as a component of the storyline (such as. flashbacks, home movies, found footage, and so on). Film grain can also add realism to shots with artificially imposed elements or CGI graphs by making them appear to have been captured on a film camera. Finally, film grain is also an aesthetic choice for many filmmakers.

> **NOTE** This exercise requires DaVinci Resolve studio to complete.

1   Turn off the timeline filter to show All Clips.

2   Switch the Node editor to Timeline mode.

By default, the Node editor appears without a node 01, which acts as a useful reminder that this stage of the grading workflow is optional and can cause significant repercussions in the appearance of the entire timeline.

3   Press Option-S (macOS) or Alt-S (Windows) to create a new serial node which will already be connected to the RGB input and node tree outputs.

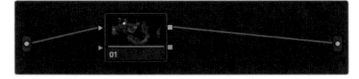

The blue outline around the node is another visual reminder that you are not in any of the standard grading node levels.

4   Label node 01 as Film Grain.

5   Open the OpenFX panel.

7   Press Shift-F to expand the viewer and have easier access to the Film Grain
     panel settings.

The top of the panel features a list of grain presets, a blending mode, and opacity
controls. Beneath it are individual settings that give you very fine control over the
grain pattern.

8   Set the Grain to 8mm 500T, and leave all other settings as they are.

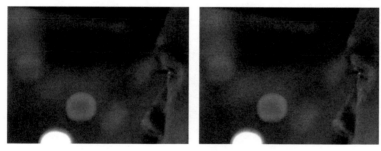

Before   After

9   Click play to review the result. All the clips on the timeline now display a prominent,
     moving grain noise. Press Shift-F to exit the full screen viewer.

10   Before moving onto the next exercise, bypass the Film Grain node. The Film Grain
     effect is processor-intensive, so it is a good idea to disable it until you are ready to
     export the project.

Adding Data Burn-in to the Viewer and Final Video

Another common feature applied on a timeline basis is data burn-In, which overlays a timecode, clip data, or any number of designated text data over the viewer. It works independent of the Node editor and you can use it in-program editorial purposes, as well as for final delivery of the video.

1   Choose Workspace > Data Burn-In.

The left side of the Data Burn-In window features a wide selection of data options that can be superimposed over the video. The right side of the interface changes depending on the option you have selected and allows you to adjust the placement of text, font, color, and so on.

The Project and Clip buttons at the top of the Data Burn-In window allow you to switch between applying the data on a timeline basis or a clip basis. This choice can be useful when you are trying to leave comments for specific clips--for example, when communicating with the audio or VFX department about the requirements of specific shots.

2   Select Record Timecode to display the timeline's timecode on the video.

3   Select Source Clip name to display the name of each clip as it plays in the video. Note that in this case, because all the clips are sourced from a single flattened video file, they will all have the same source clip name.

4   Select Custom Text1, and in the Custom Output Text field, type **The Long Work Day version 1.1**.

TIP To apply a watermark over a video, use one of the Logo options in the Data Burn-In interface. You can import a custom image/logo file and adjust its opacity using the transform controls in the Data Burn-In window.

5 Close the Data Burn-In window.

Data Burn-In options can be extremely useful for inserting quick and accurate communications between departments and clients. Instead of describing clips visually, exact clip source names can be used in feedback. Likewise, the precise timecodes ensure that your collaborators are not using the general timecodes of their video players (which usually lack frame data).

NOTE The Data Burn-In windows includes fields such as Reel Name, Shot, Take, and many others that display the information entered into those respective fields in the clips' metadata on the Media page.

By combining the knowledge you gained in previous lessons with the group-driven workflow of this lesson, you can design extremely efficient project workflows that clearly divide and allocate the purposes of each group level and node.

Self-guided Exercise

Complete the following self-guided exercises in the Project 03 - The Long Work Day Timeline to get more practice with groups, primary and secondary grading, and creative grade construction.

Home Group

- Create a Group Post-Clip grade on the Home group. Aim to create a bright, warm, saturated look, with a bit of contrast. Use HSL curves to emphasize the blue color of the sky and water outside the windows.

Highway Group

- Match the grades of the two clips in the Highway group. Pay particular attention to the color of the road in both shots.

- Apply a black-and-white look to the Highway group to match the opening clip (clip 01) on the timeline.

Office Group

- Add clips 03-05 to a new group called Office.

- Perform pre-clip group grades in the Office group. Aim to get a good luminance range that preserves detail in the midtones, while reducing the exposure issues of the lights in the room.

- Use the final clip (clip 03 in the filtered timeline) as the key shot for matching clips 01 and 02. Pay attention to the contrast and create a similar cyan shadow range on all three clips.

- Perform secondary grading on clips 01 and 03 to address the overexposed lights. If you find it difficult to adjust the exposure without affecting the rest of the image, use windows to isolate the grade.

- Perform post-clip group grades in the Office group. Aim for an overall cyan look in the lower midtones of the image, while maintaining neutral shadows and a red tint in the image gain. Return to clip mode in the Node editor to tweak any inconsistencies in the group grade.

Morning Group

- Add clips 16-18 to a new group called Morning.

- Perform pre-clip group grades in the Morning group. You can focus almost entirely on restoring the highlights in the over-exposed areas.

- Perform contrast and color matching on the clips the Morning group. Make the sunset in clip 01 (in the filtered timeline) look warmer to match the sunset in clip 02. Reduce the green and blue hues in the shadows of clip 03 to better match the preceding clips in the sequence.

- Perform post-clip group grades in the Morning group. Aim for a yellow-and-orange sunrise look. Return to clip mode in the Node editor to tweak any inconsistencies in the group grade.

When you've completed this exercise, open the Project 03 - The Long Work Day Commercial COMPLETED.drp and review the finished Lesson 8 Timeline to compare it with your work.

Lesson Review

1   True or False. A clip can belong to more than one group.

2   Which group level is ideal for performing shot matching?

3   True or False. Placing clips into groups allows you to bypass the normalizing/balancing stages of the grading workflow.

4   Which tool (and palette) can be used to quickly and accurately calibrate the starting colors and gamma of a group of clips in a scene?

5   How is data burn-in enabled?

Answers

1   False. Pre-clip and post-clip modes of the node editor apply to all the clips in a group. Removing or adding a clip to a group impacts how it is treated before and after the clip mode stage of its node editor.

2   Clip mode.

3   False. If the clips in a group do not match each other, their differences will continue to be evident when a group grade is applied.

4   A color chart and the Color Match palette.

5   Workspace > Data Burn-In.

Setting up RAW Projects

RAW media refers to a variety of still and video formats in which visual data is captured as an unprocessed video signal. In its initial state, RAW media does not have any visual properties. It is only through a processing method called 'debayering', that one is able to assign a Color space and gamma to the image to see it visually represented on the monitor. A popular choice when debayering RAW files is Log, a starting point with a wide luminance range, or Rec.709, which establishes a broadcast-standard contrast and saturation level that enables a colorist to quickly proceed with the grade.

It is ultimately up to the project objective and the colorist's personal preferences how the footage is debayered and what the starting point of the grade will be. In this lesson, you will look at three common RAW workflows.

Time

This lesson takes approximately 30 minutes to complete.

Goals

Adjusting RAW Settings at the Project Level

The DaVinci Resolve 15 color management exercises that you completed in Lesson 1 demonstrated how you can alter a project's Color space to change the starting point of a grade. Debayering RAW footage works on a similar premise, though it is a far more essential part of the grading process. Without it, the RAW media cannot be represented in the viewer.

RAW format sensors are defined by their ability to record the radiometric properties of light. Rather than ascribing a set of pixels with hard color data, RAW formats record the light intensity of a scene within the geometry of the sensor's individual photoreceptive elements, or *photo sites*.

Each photo site has a filter that allows the capture of only one channel of color (with green captured at double the frequency of red and blue). Together, the filtered signals make up the Bayer filter mosaic, which contains all the data necessary to recreate a digital image.

For this reason, RAW files are sometimes referred to as digital negatives: visual information that contains a wide dynamic range that remains unviewable until it is processed. *Debayering* (also known as *demosaicing*) allows you to appoint values to the radiometric signals and produce a visible image at a designated resolution.

Determining if Clips are RAW

You can generally recognize the RAW video file formats supported by DaVinci Resolve by their file extensions (.ari, .cin, .dng, .crm, .rmf, .nef, .r3d, and .vrw). Additionally, you can check the codec and file type of each clip in the Metadata panel of the Media page or the Clip attributes in the contextual menu.

Another quick way to verify whether footage is RAW is to place it on the timeline, and open the Camera RAW palette in the Color page. If a selected clip is in a RAW format, the palette will become active and display options for the Decode Quality and Decode Using fields. If the clip is not RAW, the Camera RAW palette is dimmed and inactive.

Color Correcting with RAW Set to Log

This setup is ideal for colorists who prefer to start grading their footage in the Log format. The initial colors may be flat and desaturated, but they still offer the full grading potential of RAW footage.

1   Open DaVinci Resolve 15.

2   Open Project 03 - The Long Work Day Commercial.

3   Enter the Media page.

4   In the Media pool, add a bin called **RAW stills** to the bin list.

5   In the Media storage library, locate the BMD 15 CC - Project 03 folder.

6   Open the RAW stills folder and drag the three RAW images into the Media pool.

7   Enter the Edit page.

8   Select the three RAW stills, right-click one, and choose New Timeline Using Selected Clips.

9   Name the timeline **Project 03 - RAW Timeline**.

A new timeline is generated containing the three RAW stills taken from the original footage of the project.

> **TIP** By default, the duration of stills introduced into a timeline is five seconds. If you wish to change this default behavior, for example, when you are working with photo-based time-lapses and wish your stills to be one frame long, you can enter DaVinci Resolve Preferences > User > Editing and amend the Standard still duration.

10 To disable the data burn-in applied in the previous lesson, open the Data Burn-In window and deselect the three data fields.

11 Enter the Color page.

> **NOTE** If smart cache is enabled in your project, the RAW stills will immediately begin the caching process. Unlike the previous media, RAW is not an intermediary codec and needs constant debayering and caching.

The color gamut of the RAW clips is currently configured by the color management you set up at the start of the project. You will be further exploring this feature later. In the meantime, you will disable it and explore the raw debayer settings alone.

12   Open Project settings.

13   In Color Management, set the Color Science to DaVinci YRGB to disable color management.

14   Switch to the Camera RAW section of the Project settings.

The Camera RAW section contains the parameters that will affect the debayering of the RAW footage on a project basis.

> **NOTE** The Camera RAW settings will affect only the RAW media and have no impact on the transcoded clips in the Project 03 - The Long Work Day Timeline.

15   Set RAW Profile to CinemaDNG.

The Decode Quality is set to Full Res. (full resolution) by default, which means that the RAW media will be debayered at the Timeline resolution specified in the Master settings. Changing the quality to Half or Quarter will substantially reduce the amount of processing required to playback the footage (at the expense of the visual quality within the viewer/monitor), but is a viable option on slower systems.

The Decode Using field allows you to specify how the color gamut of the RAW signal is debayered. By default, it is set to Camera Metadata, which is the color gamut set by the camera operator when capturing the media.

16   Leave Decode Quality at its default setting, and click Save to exit the Project settings.

17   In Project 03 - RAW Timeline, click clip 02 (A14).

To get a feel for the way grading tools behave under this gamut, you will normalize and saturate the clip to achieve a neutral starting point, mimicking the Rec.709 color gamut.

18 Drag the Lift master wheel to drop the shadows until they are just over the black point of the waveform scope.

19 Raise the Gain master wheel until the highlights on the man's shirt appear at about 90% of the waveform height.

20 Raise the Gamma master wheel to brighten the overall image.

21 Raise the Sat to 75.00.

22 Finally, on the second page of the adjustment controls, raise the MD (midtone detail) to 50.00. Doing so will increase contrast in regions of the image with high edge detail, refining their perceived sharpness.

23 Grab a still of the image, and label it Camera Metadata.

This setup method gives you a good level of control over the luminance and contrast setup of the image, but offers in a more complicated starting point for color adjustments.

Color Correcting with RAW Set to CinemaDNG Default

This workflow is reminiscent of the workflow you practiced in Lesson 1, in which you assigned a Rec.709 color gamut to a project to create a strong starting grade that complies with broadcast standards. The colors of the RAW image are remapped to an optimal dynamic range for consumer monitors with deep shadows, bright highlights and full, saturated colors.

1   Reset the grade on clip 02.

2   Open Project settings.

3   Within the Camera RAW master section, set Decode Using to CinemaDNG Default.

4   Click Save to exit the Project settings.

The image will appear significantly more contrasted and saturated, providing a more straightforward starting point for grading.

5   Once again, use the master wheels to normalize the clip. Aim to achieve a similar trace in the waveform as the one you had when grading the Camera Metadata clip.

6   In the Gallery, double-click the Camera Metadata still to activate image wipe.

Camera Metadata (Log)   CinemaDNG Default (Rec709)

Compare how differently the contrast and colors are treated during the primary color stage. A great level and variety of color is preserved in the man's skin, as well as a better representation of the range of light in the furniture and on his shirt.

7 Turn off Image wipe.

8 Zoom in on the whiskey decanter in the lower-left corner of the image.

One consequence of remapping RAW data to a dynamic Color space (such as Rec.709) is that the luminance could appear exaggerated in some areas. This can be addressed with adjustments to the highlight ranges of the image.

9 Open the custom Curves palette.

10 Place a control point in the upper midtones of the ganged YRGB curve, and drag its white point down until it reaches the first horizontal line in the curves graph.

11 Switch the viewer to Fit the screen size, or press Shift-Z.

If the curve adjustment affected the luminance of the rest of the image, tweak the position of the control point in the upper midtones to ensure the bottom half of the curve is as close to its original diagonal position as possible.

This workflow gave you a faster starting point to the grade, but, like all other grading workflows, it still required attention to detail to ensure that all colors and luminance levels were appropriate.

Adjusting RAW Settings at the Clip Level

You have another way to affect RAW footage outside of the Camera RAW Project settings: within the Camera RAW palette in the Color page, which allows tweaking on a clip-by-clip basis. The settings in the RAW palette give you greater degree of control over how a RAW image is processed and its RGB values at the input stage of the Node editor.

1   Reset the grade on clip 02.

2   In the left palettes of the Color page, open the Camera RAW palette.

3   Set Decode Using to Clip. Doing so will disconnect it from the Project settings and allow you to manipulate the RAW settings on the clip individually.

The RAW palette offers a wide variety of color and detail adjustments that are applied to the visual data of the image during debayering. The debayer level affects images before they enter the RGB input node of the Node editor.

4   Set the Color space to Blackmagic Design. The clip is now output in the Log gamut. You can use this setting to override the camera metadata in the event that the footage was not originally captured in a Log gamut.

5   Change the Color space to Rec.709. This time, the image is debayered to a
     scene-referred Rec.709 Color space, like the CinemaDNG default setting.

The Camera Raw palette gives you additional control over how the gamut and
ISO of the image is treated, allowing for optimal luminance treatment.

6   Set Gamma to Gamma 2.4.

This resulting image is now the optimal choice of the three options covered above.
It features rich, saturated colors, and a well-defined contrast, while still leaving you
plenty of room to experiment with the colors.

7   Finally, to address the lighting on the decanter, drag the Highlights field to the left
     until you can see the details on the cabinet surface.

     This tweak achieves a result that was the equivalent of adjusting the top of the
     YRGB curve in the previous exercise.

     Clip 03 (C12) has a similar gamma range to clip 02. To save time, you can re-apply
     the RAW palette settings you had just set up.

8   With clip 02 still selected, Cmd-click (macOS) or Ctrl-click (Windows) clip 03 to
     highlight it.

9   In the lower-right of the Camera RAW palette, click Use Settings.

Clip 03 is adjusted to decode using clip settings in the Rec.709 Color space at a 2.4 Gamma, and its Highlights are lowered to match clip 02.

> **TIP** If you need to adjust multiple clips on the timeline after setting up their individual RAW parameters (for example, wanting to increase the Color Boost of a sequence without overwriting the unique ISO and Highlight settings of each clip), Shift-click to select the sequence on the timeline, and click Use Changes to copy only the altered parameter.

Your final action will be to set up a RAW clip's ISO.

10   Click clip 01.

11   In the Camera RAW palette, change Decode Using to Clip to overwrite the Project Settings.

12   Set the Color space to Rec.709 and the Gamma to Gamma 2.4

One serious issue with this image is the brightness of the environment outside the shot. In a Rec.709 image, this data would be irrevocably lost. However, because the dynamic range of a RAW sensor is several f-stops beyond what can be represented in the Rec.709 color gamut of the viewer, you have exposure latitude. So, you can change the exposure levels, or ISO, after the image was recorded.

13   Change the ISO to 400.

Doing so restores the data outside the windows, while still maintaining a good luminance range in the foreground, interior portion of the image.

The Camera RAW palette is best used for establishing the color gamut and ISO of RAW media prior to grading, rather than for actual grading.

In fact, it is highly advisable to avoid balancing or creating looks in the Camera RAW palette. The standard grading tools in the Color page have the same level of impact on the raw image and are far easier to keep track of in the context of the node tree, which will reduce instances of destructive grading.

> TIP When saving stills from clips with manually adjusted Camera RAW settings, you can specify that you do not wish their camera RAW settings included in the still grade data. Right-click in the gallery and choose Copy Grade: Preserve Camera Raw Settings to enforce this.

Color Correcting with RAW Through Resolve Color Management

This technique for the color setup of a project expands on the color management concept and allows you to apply a distinct look to your footage prior to the grading stage. This workflow can be convenient for dailies workflows, as well as for projects in which the cinematographer was utilizing a custom, in-camera LUT during recording.

1   In Project 03 - RAW Timeline, click clip 02.

2   Open Project settings.

3   Enter the Color Management menu.

4   Set the Color Science to YRGB Color Managed.

5   Set the Input Color space to Bypass.

The program automatically detects raw media formats and remaps them to the Timeline and Output color spaces. Setting an Input Color space when working with raw media can clip the waveform of the debayered image, resulting in a more restricted gamut.

6   Set the Timeline and Output Color space to Gamma 2.4.

7   Click Save to exit the Project settings.

8   Return to the Camera RAW palette in the Color page.

You still have full access to the individual debayer controls of each clip. You can change the ISO, white balance, temperature, and full range of luma and color configurations.

This final option features several optimal visual solutions and grading freedoms. By employing Color Management, the raw signal's color gamut can be accurately remapped (in terms of hue, saturation, and luminance) on a timeline basis, while preserving full control over the individual raw image properties.

Following this, you can then adjust the Timeline and Output color spaces based on your intended delivery, which makes it easy to switch between gamut standards for broadcast, theatre, and web with the click of a button.

> **NOTE** If the media was captured with an in-camera LUT, you could even use the Lookup tables controls in the Color Management page to remap the color space of the image and get an approximation of the look intended by the cinematographer.

Setting up a Render Cache for RAW Media Projects

In Lesson 7, you set up a project render cache to a full-quantization format (444 or 4444) codec, but the exercise did not go into detail about how the image was impacted. In this exercise, you will reset the render cache quality and perform a simple grade test to fully understand why a render cache format matters when working with high-quality video.

1   Choose Playback > Render Cache > Smart.

2   In the Project 03 - RAW Timeline, click clip 03.

3   Open Project settings, and click the Master settings tab.

4   Scroll down to the Optimized Media and Render Cache section, and set the Render cache format to a lower-quality codec, such as ProRes 422 (macOS) or DNxHR HQ (Windows).

> **NOTE** To accurately see what the new render quality setting has on the raw media, ensure that in the Color Management settings, the Input Color Space is set to Bypass.

6   Open the Camera RAW palette, and reduce the Lift value to -20.00.

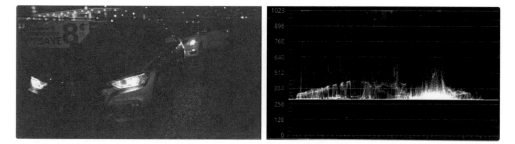

This change significantly darkens the image, leaving only the headlights and the lights in the background still visible.

In Lesson 5, you learned that, when used correctly, the node pipeline is non-destructive. So, raising the Lift master wheel or the black point of the custom curve should completely restore the crushed data in this image.

7   In the custom curves palette, drag the YRGB black point up 25%.

The result is an image with severely clipped shadows. In the waveform scope, you can see that the bottom of the trace appears flat where the Camera RAW palette crushed it during the debayering stage.

At first, it might appear that grading with raw media (or using the Camera RAW palette) results in image degradation. But actually, the rendered cache is being generated at a bit depth that is too shallow to represent the full gamut of the debayered raw image in the Viewer.

NOTE This behavior is not exclusive to the Camera RAW palette. If you construct two nodes with opposing gamma adjustments, you would see the same clipped result.

8   Open Project settings, and click the Master settings tab.

9   Set the Render cache format to one of the full-quantization (444 or 4444) or HDR formats.

10 Click Save to close the Project settings.

11 Click the custom curves black point, and adjust it slightly to force the clip to regenerate the cache.

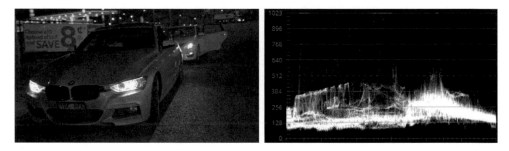

Instantly, the shadows are restored and you can see the original image data. The trace in the waveform is also restored and no longer appears flat at the bottom of the graph.

Though you did not change the Camera RAW settings or the custom curves grade, the render cache is now generated at a greater bit depth and is capable of displaying the full gamut of the restored image.

When setting a Render cache format, always remember that it affects only what you see in the viewer. If you were to render a clip from the Deliver page while caching to a low-quality codec, the exported image would not have clipped shadows and highlights. This behavior makes it particularly important to set up a high-quality cache when grading HDR and high-bit-depth footage. If you don't, your project could end up looking very different from what you are seeing in the viewer.

TIP 12-bit codecs (such as DNxHR HQX, DNxHR 444, and ProRes 4444) are HDR compliant and can be used for cinema and UHD 4K delivery.

Due to its level of quality, you can use a 12-bit cache in the final export of a project. When adjusting the Render Settings, in the Advanced Settings, select "Use render cached images".

The intermediary codecs available in the Master settings are all relatively high quality for editing and review work; but as you can see from this exercise, not all of them are suitable for grading high-quality media. Due to their lower bit depths, most codecs are incapable of displaying the full scope of your grading work, and could seriously impede the quality of your qualifier selections, and the detail in highlights and shadows.

Lesson Review

1　True or False? Enabling Resolve Color Management will not affect RAW media.

2　In which palette would you adjust a clip's individual RAW settings?

3　True or False? The Camera RAW palette gives you much finer control over the luminance ranges of RAW media than the standard grading tools in the Color Page.

4　True or False? Changes in the Camera RAW palette could permanently clip the gamma range of the image before it enters the node pipeline.

5　True or False? The ISO and white balance of RAW media can be changed at any time.

Answers

1   False. Resolve Color Management is one of the methods used to set up RAW projects.

2   Camera RAW palette.

3   3 False. The standard grading tools in the Color Page give you the same level of access to the visual properties of the image.

4   False. The Camera RAW palette is no more destructive than any of the other grading tools in the Color Page. Clipping is a possibility if you alter a range of the image and fail to retrieve it correctly at a later stage.

5   True. Due to the wide dynamic range of RAW media, it is possible to adjust the ISO and white balance in the Camera RAW settings of any clip, and at any stage of the grading process.

Lesson 10

Delivering Projects

When you're ready to export a project — whether at the end of a workflow, at an intermediate point, or when generating dailies - the render settings and final output are configured in the Deliver page of DaVinci Resolve.

This lesson will prepare a project for delivery, look over the existing presets, including outputting for digital cinema and discuss how to set up your own renders.

Using Lightbox to Check Timeline Prior to Delivery

The Lightbox is a feature in the Color page that gives you an alternative, expanded representation of the timeline. It favors a general overview of the clips in the edit over the viewer-focused layout of the standard Color page. It is particularly powerful when combined with filters, and can be used to quickly assess the grade status of the clips in the timeline.

1   Open DaVinci Resolve 15.

2   Import and launch Project 03 - *The Long Work Day Commercial COMPLETED.drp*. Relink the media if necessary.

3   Open the Lesson 10 Timeline.

4   Enter the Color page.

5   In the upper-right of the Color page, click the Lightbox button.

The Lightbox displays a full-screen representation of your project timeline from left to right, top to bottom. A timeline of the right side of the window indicates the timecode of the clips, and turns into a scrollbar when there are more clips than can fit into a single page.

The Lightbox provides a more expanded overview of the thumbnail timeline and can be helpful for colorists who find the clip timeline in the regular Color page too restrictive. With a single look, the Lightbox makes it easy to determine which clips are graded and which aren't.

6 Click the clip info button in the top left corner of the Lightbox panel to reveal each clip's information underneath it.

7 Next to the clip info button, click the show sidebar button to reveal the filtering options.

8 Click on Ungraded clips in the filter.

The timeline is reduced to just four clips. The first two clips clearly belong in the *Garage* group, but must have been overlooked during grading.

9 Select both the clips and choose Groups > Garage > Assign to Group.

The majority of the grading in the Garage group was carried out in the pre-clip and post-clip stages, which means that the two clips will immediately adopt the look of the rest of the group. They will remain in the Lightbox results until the next time you change the filter, after which their new status as graded clips will be acknowledged.

The third clip in the ungraded filter results has not been touched at all.

10 In the upper-left of the page, click the Color Controls button to open the grading palettes in the lower half of the screen.

If you are working with an external monitor, you will see a full-screen output of the selected clip in the Lightbox. This means you can continue to grade and tweak your media while in Lightbox mode.

11   Set the contrast of the interior car shot to 1.1.

The final result in the filter is the solid white matte at the end of the sequence which also doesn't require grading.

12   In the sidebar filter, select Noise Reduction.

When performing noise reduction in lesson 7, it was mentioned that disabling the noise node could facilitate a faster workflow which would require less processing.

If you use this method of performance optimization, you must remember to enable the noise nodes before outputting the project.

Click the Lightbox button in the top right corner to exit the Lightbox interface.

13 The Noise Reduction filter is still active in the timeline on the Color page. Click on the two clips one-by-one and ensure their denoise nodes are enabled.

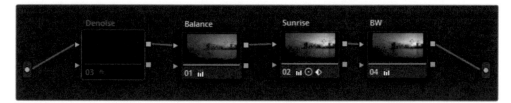

14 Select Clips > All Clips to remove the filter and return the entire timeline.

> **TIP** The timeline thumbnail mode is another great option for visually assessing the status of the clips in the timeline while in the Lightbox panel. Choose View > Timeline Thumbnail Mode > Source (C Mode) to switch the order of the clips in the timeline from their edit order, to the order in which the media was created. When working with original camera footage, this will be the order in which the footage was recorded. C Mode will place clips captured on the same day/location next to each other, which enables faster copying of grades and visual comparisons.

The media has now been checked to ensure that grades have been applied to all relevant clips and all nodes are active. When working on your own projects, think about the types of workflows you use and what is important for you to verify before delivering a project. As well as the standard filters already present in the sidebar, you can also use the smart filters option at the bottom of the list to design your filters based on the metadata of the clips on the timeline.

Understanding the Render Workflow and Presets

The Deliver page is optimally designed to help you quickly set up a render. You need perform only four steps needed to export a video from Resolve:

1   In the Render settings panel, specify the video output format. These settings include the file type, codec and audio format of the rendered video, its name and location on your workstation, and a variety of advanced controls to optimize the render speed and file size.

2   Define the range of the timeline that you want to export. By default, each render is set to render the Entire Timeline, but can be altered with in and out points to define a custom range.

3   Click Add to Render Queue to send the job to the Render Queue.

4   Click Start Render to begin the render process.

In the following exercise you will create a render job using the presets in the Project Settings of the Deliver page.

5   Enter the Deliver page.

At the top of the Render Settings panel, you will find a horizontal list of render presets.

Custom provides access to the full range of render settings.

YouTube/Vimeo sets up the render settings based on the video configurations recommended by user-generated content websites such as YouTube and Vimeo.

Prores, H.264 and H.265 Masters can be used to deliver several versions of a file for the client - from a high-end export appropriate for many projection and broadcast standards (Prores), to a compressed HD/UHD file for review or online playback (H.264 and H.265). Note, that the Prores and H.265 Masters is only available on Mac systems.

IMF features a set of SMPTE ST.2067-compliant resolutions and codec presets for tapeless deliverables to networks. It does not require a license, and supports multiple media streams for video, audio and subtitle tracks.

Final Cut Pro 7, X/Premiere XML, and AVID AAF set up the render settings to accommodate a return trip to the respective NLE software. This assumes a workflow in which media was originally edited in an NLE, migrated to Resolve for grading, and is being returned to the same NLE for final delivery.

Pro Tools renders out three files: a self-contained video file for reference, individual exports of all audio clips and their channels, and an AAF file for Avid Pro Tools migration. This preset accommodates workflows in which the final audio mix is being assembled by an external audio engineer in Pro Tools.

Audio Only will disable video output and deliver a single audio file from the timeline.

NOTE The Interoperable Mastering Format (IMF) is used for broadcast distribution and submitting content to Netflix.

Clicking the icon of a preset will reveal its settings in the Render Settings panel.

6   Click the disclosure arrow next to the YouTube preset, and choose 1080p to set up the full HD version of the preset.

By default, the filename is derived from the name of the active timeline.

7   To change the name of the exported video file, click the File section of the Project Settings.

8   Enter the custom name as **WorkDay_YouTube_1.1**.

This filename at the top of the Project settings updates with the new custom name.

9   The Location field identifies where the rendered file will be sent upon render. A job cannot be sent to the Render Queue without being assigned a location.

Click the Browse button next to the Location text field.

10 In the File Destination window, navigate to your Desktop, and click Add New folder.

11 Name it **Exports** and click OK.

Presets are convenient for quickly setting up project renders, but continue to offer customization controls for further tweaking.

12 Click the Video section of the render settings.

13 Scroll down within the panel and change the Quality to "Restrict to" 7500 Kb/s. This will reduce the data rate of the file, significantly lowering the file size while still maintaining a good level of visual quality.

14 With the render settings complete, click Add to Render Queue.

Supporting Multiple Resolution Options for User-generated Content Websites

Videos players on user-generated content (UGC) websites such as YouTube or Vimeo often offer the viewer an option to choose a video resolution. A lower-resolution video will enable smoother playback on a low-bandwidth Internet connection, whereas a higher resolution will produce a clearer image.

This change in resolution does not occur in real time within the UGC player. Instead, every resolution version of every video is generated at the time of the video's upload, which is why a wait period usually occurs before an uploaded video goes live on such sites. When switching between resolution options, the user is actually switching between separate renders of the video generated by the host website.

For this reason, it is advisable to render and upload your video in the highest quality possible and leave it up to the UGC website and the site visitor to determine which resolution is best suited for them at playback.

Using presets is an efficient way to export projects quickly, and have confidence that the settings are appropriate for the intended destination. However, it is even more valuable to understand how or why certain settings are used and to be able to configure them to more specific needs, especially when the nature of your project extends beyond the destinations targeted in the presets list.

Creating Custom Renders and Saving Presets

You begin to generate custom renders as soon as you start making changes to the fields in the Render Settings panel. Editors and colorists adjust render settings based on a wide range of factors, including the requirements of the receiving software and hardware, and the collaborative workflows they are engaging in.

In this exercise, you will set up a render job to deliver dailies to an editor who is working on a PC.

1   At the top of the Render Settings, click the Custom button.

2   Under the Filename and Location fields, choose Individual Clips. This will export every clip in the timeline as its own video file. In the case of dailies, you will want to place untrimmed clips on the timeline to ensure the editor receives the full media of every take.

3   Set the Video format to MXF OP-Atom.

4   Set the codec as DNxHD 1080p 145/120/115 8-bit.

> **TIP** Click the Delivery Full/Half button at the top of the page to expand the Render Settings panel across the Deliver page.

5   The exercises in this book did not focus on audio syncing or editing, however, it is assumed in a dailies workflow that the audio from an external recorder would have been synced to the video files. The option to export audio can remain selected under the audio tab, using the high quality Linear PCM codec.

6   Click on the File tab to configure the naming convention of the dailies.

By default, "Filename uses" is set to Custom name. When working with dailies, it is highly advisable that you preserve the original filenames (Source Name in the render settings). This will enable you to quickly switch between offline and online editing modes, as well as maintain consistency between post-production departments.

In this case, you will not want to use the source name, as all the clips have come from the same video file and will overwrite one another.

7   Enter the Custom name as **WorkDay_Dailies**.

8   Underneath, select "Use unique filenames".

9   Choose Suffix as the method in which the files will be distinguished from one another.

10   At the top of the panel, click Browse to change the Location.

11   Create a subfolder called *Dailies* within the Exports folder on the Desktop and select it as the location. Click OK to confirm.

12   In the option menu, choose Save as New Preset.

13   Name the preset **Dailies for PC**.

The custom preset appears in the horizontal menu at the top of the Render Settings panel.

14   Click Add to Render Queue.

Configuring a Timeline for Digital Cinema

A digital cinema package, or DCP, is a collection of media and metadata files used to project digital movie files in a theatrical venue. Resolve makes it convenient to create a digital cinema package with its integration of the DCP plug-in. Still, just because the process is simplified doesn't mean you needn't know what the plug-in is doing. This exercise will combine some practical information about the DCP with the few configuration steps required in the Deliver page.

When creating a DCP, the timeline in Resolve must be set to one of three 2K resolutions:

- 2K Native (1.90:1) 2048 ×1080 @ 24, 25, 30, 48, 50 and 60 fps
- 2K Flat (1.85:1) 1998 ×1080 @ 24, 25, 30, 48, 50 and 60fps
- 2K CinemaScope (2.39:1) 2048 × 858 @ 24, 25, 30, 48, 50 and 60 fps

Or one of three 4K resolutions:

- 4K Native (1.90:1) 4096 × 2160 @ 24, 25, 30, 48, 50 ,and 60 fps
- 4K Flat (1.85:1) 3996 × 2160 @ 24, 25, 30, 48, 50, and 60 fps
- 4K CinemaScope (2.39:1) 4096 ×1716 @ 24, 25, 30, 48, 50, and 60 fps

1 Ensure you are in the *Lesson 10 Timeline.*

This project is a Rec.709, full HD resolution project. But, as is often the case, you may have to output deliverables in multiple formats. In this exercise, you will output a DCP format file.

The resolution for your DCP will be 2K flat because it is the closest resolution option when starting from full HD. You will still need to scale the project up and crop some of the top and bottom.

TIP 4K DCPs use a lower bit rate when played on 2K projectors than 2K DCP's. For that reason, when your target projector is 2K, always make a 2K DCP, even if your content supports higher resolutions.

2 In the Edit page, choose File > Project settings.

3 In the Master Project settings, set the "Timeline resolution" to 1998 x 1080 DCI Flat 1.85.

4 In the Image Scaling settings, set the Input Scaling to "Scale full frame with crop".

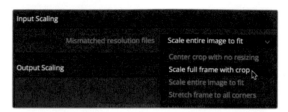

Scaling full frame with crop ensures that the shortest dimension of the source clip fills the Timeline resolution's frame to omit letterboxing or pillars. However, it does crop a small portion off the top and bottom of the image.

5　Click Save to close the window.

Your frame size is now DCP compliant. The project timeline is 24 fps, which is also appropriate for DCP delivery. However, if you had been working on a project using 23.976 fps, DCP would still interpret it as 24 fps, and audio playback would be pulled up to match.

Now you can move onto the Deliver page to set up some DCP-specific parameters.

Rendering a DCP

Once the resolution and frame rate are appropriately set up, all further output parameters are configured in the Deliver page.

The DCP plug-in in DaVinci Resolve 15 Studio features two sets of codecs: the Kadaku-based JPEG 2000 standard requires no license and delivers unencrypted digital cinema packages. The easyDCP format allows for the encryption of digital media after the acquisition of a licensing package.

1　Enter the Deliver page.

2　In the upper-left, in the Render Settings, click Custom.

3　In the Render Settings click Single Clip.

4　In the Video tab, In the Format menu, choose DCP.

5　In the Codec menu, choose Kakadu JPEG 2000 2K DCI Flat.

> TIP DCP uses the XYZ color space. The conversion of your project color space to XYZ is done during the creation of the DCP file. The project color space is determined by the timeline color space setting in the Color Management settings, even when DaVinci YRGB color management is not in use.

6 Leave the maximum bitrate at 211 Mb/sec.

7 The next checkbox determines if you are generating the DCP based on the older but more widely supported Interop standard, or the more current and feature-rich SMPTE standard. One of the benefits of using the SMPTE standard is that it supports a wider range of framerates. The major benefit of using the Interop standard is that it will work on more projects that are installed in theaters, even though it is limited to only 24 or 48fps.

Leave "Use interop packaging" selected.

> TIP When you are delivering a DCP to a film festival, you should avoid encryption. Encryption keys are linked to a specific theater and projector, so if a screening room or location is changed at the last minute, as is often the case in festivals, the encryption would prevent your project from being screened.

Naming and Outputting a DCP

DCPs follow a somewhat specific, yet voluntary, Digital Cinema Naming Convention for the content title. For each version of a movie you create (such as the English 5.1 version, the Spanish 5.1 version, the stereo version, the in-flight version, and so on), a composition play list (CPL) must be created that contains the appropriate content name. The DCP presets create this CPL for you and include a straightforward way to create a name that follows the naming convention.

1 Ensure you are still in the Video tab.

2 Scroll down the Render Settings panel to locate Composition name, and click Browse to open the DCP Composition Name Generator window.

Here, you can enter the metadata that will be used to create a content title that is compatible with DCP servers and theater management systems.

> **TIP** Separate the words in your movie's title using initial caps - not spaces, hyphens, or underscores.

3   Enter the Film Title as **TheLongWorkDay**, select the Content Type as SHR (Short Subject), and set the Audio Language to EN (English). The selected metadata is added to the composition name.

4   Delete the remainder of the composition name after the letters EN to finalize the name.

5   Click OK to close the window.

The Composition name is not to be confused with the folder name that contains the DCP. That folder name is still managed in the File tab of the Deliver page.

6   Click the File tab, and enter the Custom name as **Long Work Day DCP test**.

Lastly, you need to select a destination for this DCP.

7   Click the Browse button, and select a location in which to save your output.

You can output the DCP to a hard drive in a Cru Dataport DX-115 enclosure which will load directly onto many digital cinema servers and is often required by some film festivals. More conveniently, you can output to a USB 2 or 3 hard drive, or even a USB stick if it accommodates the film file size. No matter what storage device you choose, the device must be formatted as a Linux EXT2 or EXT3 drive. You can do so in a macOS or Windows environment by installing Linux in a virtual environment.

> **TIP** Some servers do not have enough power for some USB-powered drives to mount. In those scenarios, be sure to use a USB drive that uses an external power source.

8   When you are done selecting your drive destination, click "Add to Render Queue".

After your DCP is rendered onto the correct hard drive, you'll want to test it. The only fool-proof way to test your DCP is to rent a theater and run it just as it would be projected for an audience. That is the only way you can absolutely verify that the color conversion worked perfectly.

Using Commercial Workflow to Export Versions

In Lesson 5, one of the uses listed for versions was color experimentation. When working with clients or directors, the colorist might spend time at the beginning of the post-production workflow establishing the look of key shots, and submitting them for review and approval.

Another, practical application of sharing multiple versions of a grade involves VFX migration workflows that require reference grades to be used for reconstruction or matching. You can export these different looks or versions using a single job in the Render Queue.

1   Ensure you are in the Lesson 10 Timeline.

2   Open the Color page.

3   Right-click clip 01 and check its list of local versions.

Note that it has four versions, all featuring variants of the grade with and without color, and with and without keyframed sizing. You will export all four versions for review and approval.

4   Open the Deliver page.

5   Right-click clip 01, and choose Render This Clip to place In and Out markers around the clip in the Deliver page timeline.

> **TIP** One of the options in the Versions contextual menu is 'Render Disabled'. This will prevent a version from being rendered out during the commercial workflow.

6   In the Render Settings panel, change the render focus to Individual clips.

> **NOTE** You cannot select "Use commercial workflow" when exporting media as a single clip.

7   In the Location field, find the Exports folder on the Desktop and create a new subfolder called Sunrise Versions.

8   In the Video section of the Render Settings, specify the Format as QuickTime and the Codec as H.264 to output a compressed video with a small file size.

9   Set the resolution to Full HD (1920x1080).

10   In the Audio section, deselect the Export Audio option.

11   In the File section, ensure that "Filename uses" is set to Source Name.

12   Select "Use unique filenames" to ensure that the rendered media does not overwrite earlier versions of itself.

13   Select Suffix to place a unique identifier after the name of the clip.

14   Scroll down inside the Render Settings panel and select "Use commercial workflow". This option exports all available versions of your media.

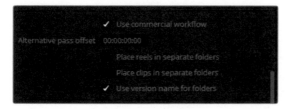

15   Select Use Version name for folders to quickly differentiate between the version types.

16   Click Add to Render Queue.

17 In the Render Queue palette, click to select the newly created job and click the Start Render button below.

Note that the other, unselected jobs will not be rendered.

18 Open your computer's file manager and locate the Sunrise Versions folder.

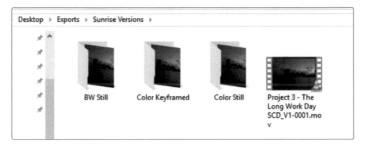

Version 1 is at the root of the folder, while all additional versions are contained in their own subfolders. You can use this structure to great effect in a workflow where version 1 is the designated ungraded version of every clip on the timeline, and the graded versions are output into their own subfolders through the commercial workflow.

Also, the subfolders themselves are vital when working with DPX file formats, which produce hundreds, or even thousands, of still images upon render.

TIP Versions also have an Enable Flat Pass option in their contextual menu. When this option is chosen, the grade on the version is disabled if Enable Flat Pass > "With clip settings" is selected in the Render Settings panel.

Exploring Advanced Render Settings

In addition to choosing how your footage is compressed, you have additional control over more nuanced aspects of the rendering process. This exercise is designed to familiarize you with these settings, and enable you to set up your custom renders with more purpose.

1 In the Render Settings, change the render focus to Single clip.

2 In the Timeline panel, set the render range to Entire Timeline.

3 In the Render Settings panel, select the Vimeo preset at 720p resolution. Leave the Video format as QuickTime and the codec as H.264.

4   Restrict the Quality setting to 4500 Kb/s. Doing so will substantially reduce the file size of the final render, albeit at the expense of its visual quality.

The Quality value in the Render Settings panel specifically refers to the bit rate of the digital data—that is, the data-per-second required to transmit the audiovisual stream. A higher bit rate moves more data which results in better color representation and detail quality, whereas a lower bit rate selectively discards some data in the interest of generating a smaller file size.

5   Restrict the Key Frames to be grabbed every 12 frames to ensure less distortion during the temporal compression and playback of the video.

Key frames are full-data, intra-coded frames, or i-frames, inserted into a lossy video stream at regular intervals, such as every 12 frames. These i-frames are reference points for recreating the temporally-compressed p- (predicted) and b- (bi-directionally predicted) frames that make up the majority of the moving image in a distribution codec.

6   Click the disclosure triangle to see the Advanced Settings options.

The "Pixel aspect ratio" allows you to indicate whether the video pixels are Square or Cinemascope. This option pertains to older workflows in which digital footage recorded for analogue television (at a rectangular 1.33:1 aspect ratio) is converted for computer displays (which have a square 1:1 aspect ratio). If your video looks horizontally distorted (too squashed, or stretched out), change the pixel aspect ratio.

7   Since you are working on digitally recorded and encoded media, you can leave the pixel aspect ratio as square.

Data Levels specify the data range of an image based on its source. The default Auto setting renders the media at the data level that is appropriate for the selected codec. Video refers to YCbCr formats that constrain to pixel data values between 64-940 on a 10-bit system in formats using a Rec.709 video standard. Full expands the range to the film standard of 4-1024 values, which is utilized in high-end digital film formats. If you find that your final video looks substantially darker or lighter than it appears in the viewer of the Color page, it is likely that the data levels are being incorrectly assigned.

8   Leave the data levels on auto.

9   Set the "Data burn-In" to None to ensure that the viewer's data burn-In information will not appear in the rendered video.

The following options — "Use optimized media" and "Use render cached images" allow you to employ previously-generated renders of the footage in the export process. It makes sense to select these options when your optimized media and render cache are set to a high or lossless quality, such as 444 or HDR.

The project is currently using a lossless render cache code, so it makes sense to use it in the final render for a faster output.

10 Select "Use render cached images".

11 Set Enable Flat Pass to "With clip settings".

This option allows you to bypass grades applied to versions of clips in the timeline. The default choice is Off, which ensures that all grades remain intact. Choosing "With clip settings"' ensures that the render will take into account the bypass status of each clip's version. Choosing Always On will disable all the grades in the timeline, providing a quick way to export an edited timeline or a set of dailies without a grade.

12 Selecting "Disable edit and input sizing" removes any transform changes that were applied to the clips in the Edit or Color pages. Leave it deselected.

The "Force sizing to highest quality" and "Force debayer to highest quality" settings both bypass the quality settings for resizing and debayering in the Project settings. Selecting one of these is convenient when working on a processor-intensive timeline that uses high-quality images or RAW footage. You can adjust the Project settings to ensure a lower-quality visual output during editing, but bypass such settings to ensure the highest possible quality output upon final render.

13 The resize filter in the Project settings hadn't been reduced to the lower bilinear format in this project, but you can still keep "Force sizing to highest quality" selected for safety.

14 You also don't need to change the debayer for this exercise because the timeline does not contain any RAW media.

15 Click Add to Render Queue.

16 In the Render Queue, in the options menu, choose Show All Projects.

You should now see all the jobs that have been added to the Render Queue in any project currently associated with the database you are using. If you split longer projects into reels, or you are working on timelines with different frames rates for the same client, you might want to access all of the jobs in the queue to render them from a single project, instead of waiting for a batch to render before launching other projects.

17 Use the options menu and deselect Show All Projects to return to the current project Render Queue.

> **TIP** In the Render Queue, double-click the job label to rename a job. When performing multiple renders, clearly labeled jobs will make it easy to keep track of what each job is doing and whether it has been completed or not.

Editing Render Jobs

Even after you add jobs to the Render Queue, you can update their settings or remove them from the queue entirely.

1 Your Render Queue still displays the Versions job, which has already been rendered out.

Click the X in the upper-right corner of the job to delete it from the queue.

2 In the Render Queue, click the pencil icon on the Vimeo job you created in the previous exercise.

The Render Settings change to reflect the settings of the Vimeo render. The presence of additional update and cancel buttons at the bottom of the render settings panel indicates that a job is currently being edited.

Change the resolution to 1920x1080 for Full HD.

3   Under that, change the Quality to Restrict to 8500 Kb/s.

4   Click Update Job at the bottom of the render settings panel to exit the edit mode.

The change overrides the original Vimeo job with the new settings.

Remote Rendering

DaVinci Resolve Studio allows you to offload rendering to another Resolve workstation. Remote rendering requires that all workstations have a copy of DaVinci Resolve 15 Studio installed, a shared Postgres database, and access to all necessary media files using the same filename path. With one computer acting as a render station, all other Resolve stations can continue to be used for further editing and grading.

Utilizing the correct render settings is vital to delivering an aesthetically correct and technically functional video project. Understanding these settings has even greater benefits. It elevates your skillset as a colorist and imbues confidence that your projects are delivered at their optimal quality and adhere to industry standards.

Lesson Review

1   Yes or no? You can continue to view and grade media in the Lightbox?

2   True or False? The Deliver page supports roundtrip workflows with other NLE programs.

3   What does the commercial workflow in the Deliver Page do?

4   How do you save a custom render preset?

5   True or False? It is possible to continue editing render jobs after they have been added to the render queue.

Answers

1   Yes, if you enable color controls and have an external monitor.

2   True. The presets at the top of the Render Settings panel allow you to select an NLE program for a roundtrip delivery of intermediary video files and an XML timeline.

3   Renders all versions of individual clip grades.

4   Render Settings options menu > Save as New Preset.

5   True. The pencil icon in the upper-right corner of a render job allows you to continue modifying its settings.

Congratulations!

You have completed **Color Correction with DaVinci Resolve 15** and are ready to explore more editing, visual effects, color grading, and audio mixing functionality using the additional certified books in this series. Completing all the lessons in this book have prepared you to become a certified DaVinci Resolve user. You can take the online exam by following the link below to earn your certificate.

We also invite you to become part of the DaVinci Resolve community by joining the web forum on the Blackmagic Design web site. There, you can ask further questions about the creative aspects of editing, color correction and audio mixing.

We hope that you have you have found DaVinci Resolve 15's professional non-linear editing and world-class color correction tools to be intuitive to learn and a perfect fit to become the hub of your entire creative workflow.

Test your skills by taking the online assessment: **http://bit.ly/2Nwi8ii**

Setting Up and using the Blackmagic Design Mini Panel

Using DaVinci Resolve Panels

The DaVinci Resolve Panels allow you to make incredibly detailed, subtle, and nuanced changes to the color of your images. Instead of being limited to color grading one click or drag at a time, the panels let you effect multiple controls in different direction at the same time. It could be the difference between taking one minute and five minutes to complete a shot before moving on to the next.

The role of the colorist isn't only about creativity, it's about efficiency. To meet the time requirements of your budget as well as the expectations of your client, you'll have to find ways to quickly save, copy, apply, and tweak numerous looks throughout your projects. Having a set of panels will help you meet those time-sensitive demands.

DaVinci Resolve Mini Panel

The DaVinci Resolve Mini Panel is a compact panel that's packed with a massive combination of features and controls. As with the Micro Panel, you get three professional trackballs along with a variety of buttons for switching tools, adding color correctors, and navigating your node tree. In addition to every tool and feature available on the Micro Panel, the Mini Panel features two 5" color LCD screens that display menus, controls, and parameter settings for the selected tool, along with 8 soft buttons and 8 soft knobs that give you direct access to the menus for specific features. The Mini Panel is ideal for users who regularly switch between editing and color grading, users who wish to access both primary and secondary color correction tools from their panel, or for freelance colorists who need to carry a panel with them when moving between facilities. It's also great for colorists working on location shoots, for corporate and event videographers, for houses of worship, and more.

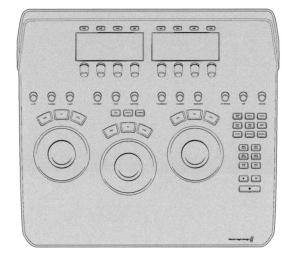

DaVinci Resolve Micro Panel

The DaVinci Resolve Micro Panel is a high-quality, portable, low-profile panel that features three high-resolution trackballs and 12 precision-machined control knobs for accessing essential primary correction tools. If you're using a Micro Panel, it's important to know that all of the instructions regarding the primary color tools and setup are identical to the Mini Panel. Above the center trackball are keys for switching between Log and offset color correction, as well as a key to display DaVinci Resolve's full-screen viewer, which is great for use with laptops. Eighteen dedicated keys on the right side of the panel also give you access to many commonly used grading features and playback controls. The Davinci Resolve Micro Panel is perfect for anyone that needs a truly portable solution. It's great for use on set to quickly create looks and evaluate color, it's ideal for grading in broadcast trucks, excellent for education, and ideal for anyone who's work relies mostly on the primary color correction tools.

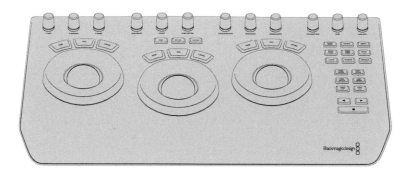

DaVinci Resolve Advanced Panel

For the ultimate in speed, power and control, there is the DaVinci Resolve Advanced Panel. The Advanced Panel has been designed in collaboration with professional colorists to work together in total harmony with the software. This large panel consists of left, center, and right consoles that give you quick, one touch access to virtually every parameter and control in the software. The DaVinci Resolve Advanced Panel lets colorists instinctively reach out and touch every part of the image, adjusting multiple parameters simultaneously with complete responsiveness for a smooth grading experience. While the Mini Panel gives you access to nearly all of the color correction tools in Davinci Resolve, the Advanced Panel gives you even more flexibility with physical buttons and knobs to control Memories, OpenFX tools, Dolby Vision HDR, and many other speed and workflow based tools that will increase your efficiency even more. The Advanced Panel also features a unique T-Bar used for playing back gallery stills, shuttle controls for cycling through frames and speeding through your timeline, as well as a slide out keyboard. Used in many of the top color grading facilities across the world, the Davinci Resolve Advanced Panel is the ultimate control surface for Davinci Resolve.

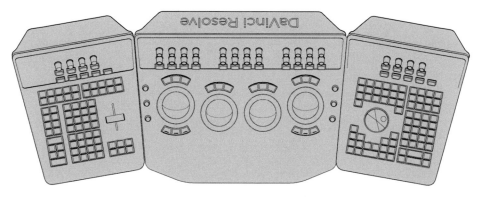

DaVinci Resolve Mini Panel Overview

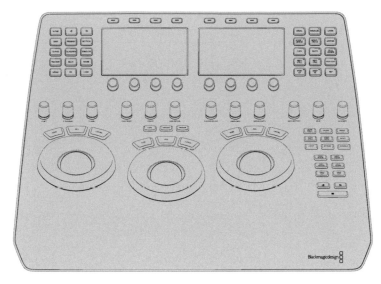

The lower-half of your Mini Panel contains the primary control tools. These tools are identical to the Micro Panel. The largest controls on the Mini Panel are the three wheels and three trackballs that control (from left to right) Lift, Gamma, and Gain. Whereas the wheel controls brightness, the trackball controls color. Look at the Color wheel on your user interface as you move the trackballs and wheels. When you move the Lift wheel to the left, the darker areas of your image grow darker. When you move the Gain trackball to the upper-left, you'll notice that the brighter areas of your image become warmer.

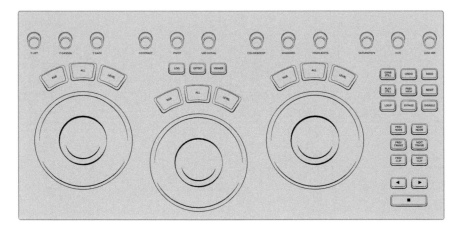

Above the Lift, Gamma, and Gain controls are your Primary knobs, which control the Primary sliders below your Color wheel in the user interface. They control frequently used Resolve tools such as Contrast, Pivot, Saturation, Color Boost, and Hue. These knobs (as well as all knobs on the panel) have 4,098 points per turn, and you can push them in to reset the tool they control.

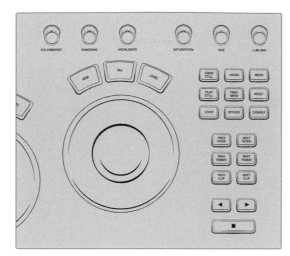

To the right of your Gain trackball and wheel, you'll find useful playback and shuttle controls to help you navigate quickly between clips, nodes, frames, and playback options. Some important controls to remember are Loop, which will loop the currently selected clip; Bypass, which will temporarily bypass all of the nodes/color corrections applied to a shot; and Disable which will temporarily disable the current node selected on a clip.

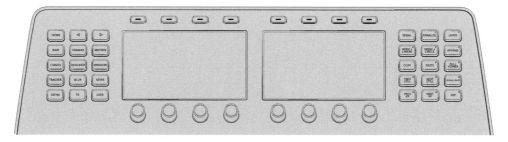

The lip of the Mini Panel consists of your tool palettes; two five-inch high-resolution displays; and even more node, keyframing and selection controls. The color tools in Davinci Resolve are accessed in the user interface through a series of icons between the timeline and color tools. All of these tool palettes are mirrored into their own buttons on the Mini Panel. If you need to access curves, just press Curves. The two displays—as well as the eight soft buttons and eight soft knobs above and below the displays—will control and manipulate whatever palette button you have selected to the left of them.

About the Author

Daria Fissoun is a colorist and compositor in east London. She specialises in commercial video projects (past clients include Microsoft, Nike, and Konami) and has worked on a number of short and feature films through UK-based production companies.

Alongside industry work, Daria is also involved in the educational sector. She currently instructs on a variety of post production topics, including compositing, motion graphic animation, and color grading. She has been a staff member or guest lecturer at film and media schools throughout London: SAE Institute London, MET Film School, Central Film School and London South Bank University. In her spare time, she records and uploads video tutorials on post production techniques in Davinci Resolve under her channel name *Goat's Eye View*.

WATCH IN DIGITAL HD FOR 50% OFF! www.airplanesmovie.com/resolve14

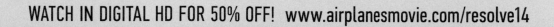

Made in the USA
Coppell, TX
10 January 2020

14326691R00197